THE LOVES OF FRANZ KAFKA

THE LOVES OF FRANZ KAFKA

Nahum N. Glatzer

Schocken Books

NEW YORK

First published by Schocken Books 1986

10 9 8 7 6 5 4 3 2 1   86 87 88 89

Copyright © 1986 by N. N. Glatzer

Library of Congress Cataloging in Publication Data
Glatzer, Nahum Norbert, 1903–
    The loves of Franz Kafka.
    Bibliography: p.
    1. Kafka, Franz, 1883–1924—Relations with women.
    2. Authors, Austrian—20th century—Biography.
    I. Title.
PT2621.A26Z7337 1985   833'.912   85–2483

Manufactured in the United States of America
Design by Leslie Phillips
ISBN 0–8052–4001–2

Acknowledgments for all copyright material used are given on page 85
which constitutes an extension of this copyright page.

Publisher's Note

Dr. Nahum N. Glatzer was recognized last year with the Jewish Museum–sponsored Kenneth B. Smilen Award for lifetime contribution to Jewish literature. He is on the editorial board of the German Historical-Critical Edition of the Complete Works of Franz Kafka presently in progress.

Born in Lemberg, Austria, in 1903, the distinguished Frankfurt University–educated scholar held Martin Buber's former chair of Jewish Philosophy and Ethics in 1932, one year before fleeing to Palestine with his wife Anne. An editor for the original Schocken Verlag since 1928, Dr. Glatzer rejoined Schocken in New York, where he co-edited his first English Kafka manuscript with Hannah Arendt in 1945.

Currently University Professor on the faculty of Boston University and a Fellow of the American Academy of Arts and Sciences, Dr. Glatzer holds doctoral degrees from the University of Frankfurt, Brandeis University, the University of Southern California, and the University of Florida. Dr. Glatzer is Professor Emeritus at Brandeis University. A Festschrift in his honor lists over 260 titles by Dr. Glatzer.

Martin Buber once wrote of the student who was to become Schocken Books' most respected and beloved senior editor, "What this younger friend has taught me was the superb combination of faith and a sense of humor."

Schocken Books is honored to publish Dr. Glatzer's magnificent labor of love in his 83rd year, *The Loves of Franz Kafka.*

Contents

Preface

The question we ask ourselves is whether Franz Kafka knew what love is. His reply: "Love is everything that enhances, widens, and enriches our life" (Janouch, *Conversations with Kafka*, 102). A fine thought, but Kafka's life was much more complicated, ambivalent—and tragic.

The story of Kafka's loves reveals that his own experiences over the course of time required a radical and in many points painful correction of an optimistic view; it culminates in the sorry admission that he has never known the words "I love you" (*Diaries* II, 221).

On the whole, Kafka's view of women was rather negative and pessimistic. To Max Brod, he wrote: "It is strange how little sharpsightedness women possess; they only notice whether they please, then whether they arouse pity, and finally, whether you look for compassion from them. That is all; come to think of it, it may even be enough, generally speaking" (*Letters to Friends*, 280). Here Kafka is speaking of the women in his stories, but since he is reacting to Brod, who spoke of "real girls" he, too, may have had real women in mind.

Kafka knew very well that love is a complex phenomenon and that it becomes more complex over time. He mentions a visit by the writer Albert Ehrenstein, who said in effect that, in Milena, "life was reaching out its hand to me and I had the choice between life and death. That was somewhat too magniloquent (not in regard to M. but in regard to me), but in essence it was true. It was only stupid in that he seemed to believe I had such a choice. If there were still a Delphic oracle, I would have asked it and it would have answered: 'The choice between death and life? How can you hesitate?' " (*ibid.*, 279f.). It was Milena who believed she could cure Kafka of all his ills and give him a sense of well-being simply by her presence—if only he wanted it. Kafka rejected the generous offer.

Recalling an encounter with a woman some years before, Kafka noted: "The sweetness of sorrow and of love. [. . .] Always only the desire to die and the not-yet-yielding; this alone is love" (*Diaries* I, 305). Such romantic notions of love should not astonish us. That love is as strong as death was known to the poet who wrote the Song of Songs ages ago. In the extra-romantic world, one would expect love to awaken life, to renew the spirit, to be a promise of eternity. To hold that love implies "the desire to die" is not an unusual thought in Kafka but striking nevertheless.

Why did Kafka not marry? He tried to explain his view to his father. "There were individual obstacles, as there always are, but then, life consists in facing such obstacles. The essential obstacle, however, which is, unfortunately, independent of the individual case, is that obviously I am mentally incapable of marrying. This manifests itself in the fact that from the moment I make up my mind to marry I can no longer sleep, my head burns day and night, life can no longer be called life, I stagger about in despair. It is not actually worries that bring this about; true, in keeping with my sluggishness and pedantry countless worries are involved in all this, but they are not decisive; they do, like worms, complete the work on the corpse, but the decisive blow has come from else-where. It is the general pressure of anxiety, of weakness, of self-contempt" (*Letter to His Father*, 111f.).

In his diaries, Kafka noted a different reason for his bachelor-hood, one that he did not wish to discuss with his father: "The hardships of living together. Forced upon us by strangeness, pity, lust, cowardice, vanity, and only deep down, perhaps, a thin little stream worthy of the name of love, impossible to seek out, flashing once in the moment of a moment" (*Diaries* II, 157). His experiences of living together did not satisfy his longing for love, however one wishes to interpret the word. At the base of it is the deep awareness of "belonging together." Kafka used the term "belong together" in addressing his beloved. If this is more than a polite form, it expresses a profound wish for love and not just a "thin trickle of a brook." Kafka knew (and enjoyed) the lower forms of love (where even the use of the word "love" is inappropriate), a relationship that can be easily entered into and painlessly termi-nated. He aspired to the higher (even highest) rank of love, where a true union is established and manifested. This was not granted to him. His guilt feelings were in a measure connected with this lack of success as a lover.

Whatever you receive in life you must be ready to pay for; this is an iron rule of this world. "Being together" brings happiness—Kafka experienced this in several of his friendships—but at what price? The price (or "punishment") for his happiness: coitus. There is no harsher, no more damning attitude to sexual embrace in Western literature. In order to avoid further punishment, Kafka counsels himself: "Live as ascetically as possible, more ascetically than a bachelor that is the only possible way for me to endure marriage" (*ibid.*, I, 296). Then he turns his attention to whoever would be his partner and asks: "But she?" He does not answer his question—for there is no answer.

To Max Brod, Kafka wrote, "You are right in saying that the deeper realm of real sexual life is closed to me; I too think so." Not only the realm of love, but "also family life, friendship, marriage, profession, literature."

In his diaries, Kafka noted a different reason for his bachelor-hood, one that he did not wish to discuss with his father: "The hardships of living together. Forced upon us by strangeness, pity, lust, cowardice, vanity, and only deep down, perhaps, a thin little stream worthy of the name of love, impossible to seek out, flashing once in the moment of a moment" (*Diaries* II, 157). His experiences of living together did not satisfy his longing for love, however one wishes to interpret the word. At the base of it is the deep awareness of "belonging together." Kafka used the term "belong together" in addressing his beloved. If this is more than a polite form, it expresses a profound wish for love and not just a "thin trickle of a brook." Kafka knew (and enjoyed) the lower forms of love (where even the use of the word "love" is inappropriate), a relationship that can be easily entered into and painlessly terminated. He aspired to the higher (even highest) rank of love, where a true union is established and manifested. This was not granted to him. His guilt feelings were in a measure connected with this lack of success as a lover.

Whatever you receive in life you must be ready to pay for; this is an iron rule of this world. "Being together" brings happiness—Kafka experienced this in several of his friendships—but at what price? The price (or "punishment") for his happiness: coitus. There is no harsher, no more damning attitude to sexual embrace in Western literature. In order to avoid further punishment, Kafka counsels himself: "Live as ascetically as possible, more ascetically than a bachelor that is the only possible way for me to endure marriage" (*ibid.*, I, 296). Then he turns his attention to whoever would be his partner and asks: "But she?" He does not answer his question—for there is no answer.

To Max Brod, Kafka wrote, "You are right in saying that the deeper realm of real sexual life is closed to me; I too think so." Not only the realm of love, but "also family life, friendship, marriage, profession, literature."

The one exception to this bleak lovelessness was Kafka's relationship with his youngest sister, Ottla. She best understood him, appreciated his writing, and had compassion for his illnesses. His letters to her are tender and loving, caring. At times they lived together; on occasional walks they took, they looked like a bridal pair. If we can say that Kafka ever loved deeply, then that love was not a romantic one but his unreserved love for Ottla.

In one of the comparative lists for and against marriage, Kafka records in the bachelor column of the list "I remain chaste." And in the opposite column, just a question: "chaste?" (*Dearest Father*, 211). Not even chastity evoked in him an enthusiastic "Yes."

Toward the end of his life, Kafka asked himself: "What have you done with your gift of sex? It was a failure, in the end that is all that they will say." But, he continues, "it might easily have succeeded. A mere trifle, indeed so small as not to be perceived, decided between its failure and success" (*Diaries* II, 203). If it was "a mere trifle" that made Kafka fail to accept "the gift of sex," it must have been something that lay in his power to act or passively to reject. Did he wish to fail?

Kafka considered his love life a dismal failure. It is known how lonely he was; the closest relatives, the best friends were unable to relieve him of the most strongly felt aloneness. They were all strangers to him; his very body was strange to him. The woman was the only being from whom he longingly anticipated liberation from this dreadful sense of isolation. But love was not strong enough to overcome his loneliness, while his loneliness was too strong to allow the growth of love.

Though Kafka was much occupied with the erotic element and with sexual fantasies in his prose, the decision was made not to include a presentation of this material in the present volume, but to concentrate on his actual experiences as he recorded them in his diaries and letters, and as recounted in Max Brod's biography of Kafka.

I am grateful to those who were helpful in various ways: Jürgen Born, Beverly Colman, Bonny Fetterman, Sir Malcolm Paisley, Wolfgang A. Schocken (no relation to the publishers), Dr. Benson R. Snyder, Paul E. Guay, Irene D. Williams, and my daughter, Judith Wechsler.

Key to Abbreviations

B Max Brod, *Franz Kafka: A Biography*. Trans. by G. Humphreys Roberts and Richard Winston. Second ed. New York: Schocken Books, 1963.

DF Franz Kafka, *Dearest Father: Stories and Other Writings*. Trans. by Ernst Kaiser and Eithne Wilkins. New York: Schocken Books, 1954.

DI Franz Kafka, *Diaries: 1910–1913*. Ed. by Max Brod. Trans. by Joseph Kresh. New York: Schocken Books, 1948.

DII Franz Kafka, *Diaries: 1914–1923*. Ed. by Max Brod. Trans. by Martin Greenberg and Hannah Arendt. New York: Schocken Books, 1949.

F Franz Kafka, *Letters to Felice*. Ed. by Erich Heller and Jürgen Born. Trans. by James Stern and Elisabeth Duckworth. New York: Schocken Books, 1973.

J Gustav Janouch, *Conversations with Kafka*. Introduction by Max Brod. Trans. by Goronwy Rees. New York: Frederick A. Praeger, 1953. Reprinted by permission of New Directions Publishing Company, publishers of Gustav Janouch. *Conversations with Kafka*. Copyright © 1968, 1971 by Fischer Verlag GmbH, Frankfurt-am-Main.

L Franz Kafka, *Letters to Friends, Family, and Editors*. Trans. by Richard and Clara Winston. New York: Schocken Books, 1977.

LF Franz Kafka, *Letter to His Father*. Trans. by Ernst Kaiser and Eithne Wilkins. New York: Schocken Books, 1966.

M Franz Kafka, *Letters to Milena*. Ed. by Willi Haas. Trans. by Tania and James Stern. New York: Schocken Books, 1965.

THE LOVES OF FRANZ KAFKA

Early Experiences

A young friend (F.W.), an unhappy lover, committed suicide. Kafka discussed the affair with his friend Gustav Janouch and during the discussion came to the question, What is love? "This is quite simple. It has as few problems as a motorcar. The only problems are the driver, the passengers, and the road" (J, 102).

"Quite simple"? Not really, if the driver, the passengers, and the road can present problems of not insignificant urgency. Not quite simple, indeed, if one recalls for a moment Kafka's unusually strong aversion to filth *(Schmutz)*. Informed of a young boy who was raped by his French governess, Kafka opined, "Love always inflicts wounds which never heal, because love always appears hand in hand with filth. Only the will of the loved one can divide love from filth" (J, 102). It is by more than implication that Kafka here blames the woman for the element of impurity in love.

Kafka always goes beyond the esthetic aspect of love. "Women are snares which lie in wait for man on all sides, in order to drag them into the merely finite. They lose their dangers if one voluntarily falls into one of the snares. But if, as a result of habit, one overcomes it, then all the jaws of the female trap open again" (J, 101f.).

3

Late in his life, in 1922, Kafka made the sad confession that he has never known the words "I love you" but "only the expectant stillness that should have been broken by my 'I love you'—that is all that I have known, nothing more" (DII, 221). Erich Heller, who quotes this diary entry at the conclusion of his introductory essay to the English edition of *Letters to Felice*, reflects, "It is the languid minnesong of a poet to whom, because there is no God, even love denies itself—or whose love is so irresistibly drawn into the empty upper spheres that it misses its earthly assignation with the beloved, just as Kafka, in the astonishingly precise fantasies he records in his New Year 1912–13 letter, misses his appointment with Felice" (F, xxiii).

Kafka was ill prepared for an "earthly assignation with the beloved." "As a boy I was as innocent of and uninterested in sexual matters [. . .] as I am today in, say, the theory of relativity. Only trifling things (yet even these only after they were pointedly called to my attention) struck me, for example that it was just those women on the street who seemed to me most beautiful and best dressed who were supposed to be bad" (DII, 227).

In the last period of his life, Kafka remembers "the first night." "We lived at that time in the Zeltnergasse, opposite a dress shop, in the door of which a shopgirl used to stand. Upstairs I, a little more than twenty years old, walked incessantly up and down the room, occupied with the nerve-racking cramming of, to me senseless, facts required for my first State examination. It was summer, very hot, quite unbearable, I stopped each time by the window, the disgusting Roman Law between my teeth, finally we came to an understanding by sign language. I was to fetch her at 8 P.M., but when I came down in the evening someone else was already there. [. . .] Although the girl took his arm she nevertheless signed to me that I should follow them. Thus we arrived at the Schützen Island where we drank beer, I at the next table; then we walked, I following slowly, to the girl's apartment, somewhere near the

Franz Kafka as a Doctor of Law, 1906

Fleischmarkt; there the man said goodbye, the girl ran into the house; I waited a while until she came out again, and then we went to a hotel on the Kleinseite. Even before we got to the hotel all this was charming, exciting, and horrible, in the hotel it wasn't different. And when, toward morning (it was still hot and beautiful) we walked home over the Karlsbrücke I was actually happy, but this happiness came from the fact that at last I had some peace from the ever-yearning body; above all it came from the relief that the whole experience hadn't been *more* horrible, *more* obscene.

"I was with this girl once again (two nights later, I believe), everything went as well as the first time, but as I then left immediately for the summer holidays where I played around a bit with another girl, I could no longer look at the shopgirl in Prague, not another word did I exchange with her; she had become (from my point of view) my bitter enemy, and yet she was a good-natured, friendly girl, she followed me all the time with her uncomprehending eyes. I won't say that the sole reason for my enmity was the fact (I'm sure it wasn't) that at the hotel the girl in all innocence had made a tiny repulsive gesture (not worthwhile mentioning), had uttered a trifling obscenity (not worthwhile mentioning), but the memory remained—I knew at that instant that I would never forget it and simultaneously I knew, or thought I knew, that this repulsiveness and smut, though outwardly not necessary, was inwardly however very necessarily connected with the whole thing, and that this repulsiveness and obscenity (whose little symptom had only been her tiny gesture, her trifling word) had drawn me with such terrible power into this hotel, which otherwise I would have avoided with all my remaining strength" (M, 163f.).

One would have hoped that the experience of the "first night" had brought Kafka a sense of relief, a sense of distinction between what is desirable and what is not. Rather, we see him torn and unable to come to a decision.

The description of "the first night" is followed in the letter to Milena by the statement that "as it was then, so it had always remained. My body, sometimes quiet for years, would then again be shaken to the point of not being able to bear it by this desire for a small, a very specific abomination, for something slightly disgusting, embarrassing, obscene; even in the best that existed for me there was something of it, some small nasty smell, some sulfur, some hell. This urge had in it something of the eternal Jew, being senselessly drawn, wandering senselessly through a senselessly obscene world" (M, 164).

Almost in passing, Kafka mentions that during his stay in Meran (1920) he made—against his own clear will—day-and-night plans to seduce the chambermaid, and that "a very willing girl ran across my path" (M, 164f.). "Girls" are very much on the mind of Kafka. Among the "five guiding principles on the road to hell" of 1922, one goes: "You must possess every girl!" (DII, 226), which was a guiding principle on the road to heaven in the minds of many artists and intellectuals of the time. Much earlier, in 1910, he had recorded having passed by a brothel "as though past the house of a beloved" (DI, 11), a sentiment not unusual among his contemporaries.

What distinguishes Kafka from most of his contemporaries is that none of these experiences brought him peace of mind, bliss, or satisfaction. Exceptions were his acquaintance with an unnamed woman in Zuckmantel (Silesia) in the summers of 1905 and 1906 ("she was a woman and I was a boy" [L, 117]) and his brief, intense friendship with "G.W.," a Swiss girl whom he met in 1913 in a sanatorium in Riva on Lake Garda (DI, 301ff.). "With F. [Felice Bauer] I never experienced (except in letters) that sweetness one experiences in a relationship with a woman one loves, such as I had in Zuckmantel and Riva" (DII, 112). The lovers in Riva promised to keep their affair a secret; thus we do not even know her name. They never met again, never wrote to each other. The warm glow continued, at least in the life of Kafka. Rarely does a soft, lyric tone interrupt the melancholy or downright sad melody. "I incline to the belief that the girls sustain us because they are so light; that is why we have to love the girls and why they should love us" (L, 12). The forty-year-old writer says, looking back: "What have you done with your gift of sex? It was a failure, in the end that is all that they will say. But it might easily have succeeded. [. . .] Sex keeps gnawing at me, hounds me day and night" (DII, 203f.).

Flora Klug
and Mania Tschissik

In the years 1911 and 1912, Prague Jewry hosted a Jewish theater group from Eastern Europe that gave performances of Yiddish drama and song. Café Savoy, where the performances took place, was a rather dingy, shabby, and uninviting place, and the plays second-rate, if that. Kafka was a frequent visitor. What attracted him was the authentic, genuine presentation of some Jewish aspects of life in Eastern Europe and its reading of the past. An additional attraction was the presence among the actors of Mrs. Flora Klug and Mrs. Mania Tschissik. Kafka describes Mrs. Tschissik as having "protuberances on her cheeks near her mouth. Caused in part by hollow cheeks as a result of the pains of hunger, childbed, journeys, and acting, in part by the relaxed unusual muscles she had to develop for the actor's movements of her large, what originally must have been a heavy, mouth. [. . .] She has a large, bony, moderately robust body and is tightly laced. [. . .] Especially when she sang the Jewish national anthem, gently rocked her large hips and moved her arms, bent parallel to her hips, up and down with hands cupped as though she were playing with a slowly flying ball" (DI, 106).

"The striking smoothness of Mrs. Tschissik's cheeks alongside her muscular mouth. Her somewhat shapeless little girl" (DI, 108). Kafka speaks of his "love for Mrs. Tschissik"—"I enjoy writing the name so much"(DI, 107)—we do not see why but must believe it was true love. "Mrs. Tschissik was beautiful yesterday," Kafka notes. "The really normal beauty of small hands, of light fingers, of rounded forearms which in themselves are so perfect that even the unaccustomed sight of this nakedness does not make one think of the rest of the body" (DI, 139).

The next possible town for the Yiddish group to perform in was discussed in the presence of Kafka, who took occasion to look at Mrs. Tschissik. "All that part of her body which was visible above the table, all the roundness of shoulders, back, and breast, was soft despite her [. . .] bony, almost coarse build" (DI, 141f.).

At one of the last performances Kafka brought along a bouquet for Mrs. Tschissik, with an attached card inscribed "in gratitude," and waited for the moment when he could have it presented to her. The play dragged on, and Kafka was afraid the flowers might wilt; he asked the waiter to present the flowers as early as possible. "They lay on a table, the kitchen help and several dirty regular guests handed them from one to another and smelled them. I could only look on worried and angrily, nothing else; I loved Mrs. Tschissik. [. . .] The headwaiter handed up the flowers, Mrs. Tschissik took them between final curtains. [. . .] No one noticed my love; I had intended to reveal it to all and so make it valuable in the eyes of Mrs. Tschissik; the bouquet was hardly noticed" (DI, 134f.). "I had hoped, by means of the bouquet of flowers, to appease my love for her a little; it was quite useless. It is possible only through literature or through sexual intercourse. I write this not because I did not know it, but rather because it is perhaps well to write down warnings frequently" (DI, 137). The following day the actors left Prague.

Kafka was less attracted to another important actress in the Yiddish group: Mrs. Klug, who appeared as "male impersonator." She wore "a caftan, short black trousers, white stockings; from the black vest a thin white woolen shirt emerges that is held in front of the throat by a knot and then flares into a white, loose, long, spreading collar. On her head, containing her woman's hair but necessary anyhow and worn by her husband as well, a dark, brimless skullcap, over it a large, soft black hat with a turned-up brim" (DI, 79). Comparing her with last year's guest artist (a Mrs. W.), Kafka finds Mrs. Klug's personality "a trifle weaker and more monotonous; to make up for it, she is prettier and more respectable" (DI, 86).

When the group left Prague Kafka and Yitzhak Levy, a Yiddish actor who had become Kafka's friend, "ran alongside the train and saw Mrs. Klug looking out from the darkness behind a closed window in the last coach. She quickly stretched her arm toward us while still in her compartment, stood up, opened the window, filling it for a moment with her unbuttoned cloak. [. . .] I could not, during the weak, uninterrupted conversation, turn my eyes from her. She was completely under the domination of my presence, but more in her imagination than in reality. [. . .] While I was respected by her as a person, as a spectator I was even more respected. I beamed when she sang, I laughed and looked at her all the time while she was on the stage, I sang the tunes with her, later the words, I thanked her after several performances; because of this, again, she naturally liked me very well" (DI, 126f.).

The actress had to exert herself to reward Kafka, the faithful spectator, and she was glad to do it "because she was a vain actress and a good-hearted woman." "She must have believed I loved her—as was indeed true—and with these glances she gave me the sole fulfillment that a young but experienced woman, a good wife and mother could give to the 'doctor' of her imagination" (DI, 127).

Between the two leading ladies, Kafka gave preference to Mrs. Tschissik. Once, during a talk with Mrs. Klug, Mrs. Tschissik joined the two. Kafka turned his attention to the latter, excusing himself from the other lady, "as though I intended to spend the rest of my life with Mrs. Tschissik." Then, while he was speaking to

Kafka with his sister, Ottla, 1914

Mrs. Tschissik, he observed that his love "had not really grasped her, but only flitted about her, now nearer, now farther. Indeed it can find no peace" (DI, 184).

Beyond the special charm that the young actress displayed and which affected the extremely sensitive Franz Kafka, what was it that drew him to the presence of these youngsters? After all, there was the difference of language: their German moved on a rather low level; Kafka's Yiddish was quite limited (though he himself had a higher opinion of his linguistic facilities). The plays were too sentimental and overly dramatized. What was it that made Kafka work to help prepare the performances, publicize the troupe, and attend (often with Max Brod) the plays? There may be more than one answer, and all may be only partly right or altogether wrong. Still, could it possibly be that the members of this group, who had liberated themselves from the narrow limits of life in the Jewish quarters of Eastern Europe, captivated Kafka who strove for a similar liberation from the narrowness of his parental home and an overpowering father? The actors, then, conveyed a sense of freedom, away from a world that so scrupulously distinguished between what is allowed and forbidden, socially accepted or rejected—a world where religious beliefs imposed on the adherent a more or less strict code of behavior, where it was a matter of courage to become an outsider. Kafka hungered for such liberation, and the ladies Tschissik and Klug represented such liberated personalities. Their parental homes and their towns of origin still adhered to ancient traditions, rituals, customs, folkways, but the Tschissiks and Klugs—the writers, actors, musicians, artists— though they may have experienced the sweetness and beauty of that life, broke with this old world and eagerly entered the new, remaining outsiders, people living at the outskirts of the new civilization. Women especially were good examples of this new spirit.

To be in love with them was a sign of identification with their cause, a protest against the well-ordered, restrictive theory and practice of love in the bourgeois society. That Kafka's love for the actresses was not responded to, did not bother the young Western writer as long as he was not rejected. Kafka found a similar situation in his friend Yitzhak Levy. He was liberated from his East European town and family. The pious father was no example for the son. The son, his heart filled with tradition and folkways, wished ardently to become Westernized. The road to becoming a Westerner, he thought, was to reject the old ways. Levy achieved his liberation by becoming an actor, though a minor one on a second-rate stage performing before an indifferent audience. Kafka's striving for liberation was of an immeasurably more serious kind. The Yiddish actors served as symbols, the young women as metaphors for the mature woman of the West.

Felice Bauer
and Grete Bloch

August 13, 1912: an important date in Kafka's life. A meeting in the family home of Max Brod with Felice Bauer of Berlin became the source of much joy and much despair during the next five years of Kafka's life. Felice Bauer, then twenty-four years old, was an executive secretary *(Prokuristin)* in a firm manufacturing dictating machines and sound-recording equipment. She had come to Prague on business. She was distantly related to the Brods, being a cousin of the husband of Max's sister, Sophie. Kafka had come to Brod to deliver a volume of his stories *(Meditations)*, to be given its final sequence before submitting it to the publisher. Kafka remembered the smallest details of that meeting.

When he arrived, Felice was sitting at the table. He was not curious enough to inquire who she was, but took her for granted. Her face did not attract him. It was "a bony, empty face that wore its emptiness openly" (DI, 268).

The diaries continue: "Bare throat. A blouse thrown on. Looked very domestic in her dress, although, as it later turned out, she by no means was. [. . .] Almost broken nose. Blond, somewhat straight, unattractive hair, strong chin." As he was taking his seat, "I looked at her closely for the first time, by the time I was seated I already had an unshakable opinion" (DI, 268f.). And what was his "unshakable opinion"? The context does not suggest a positive one; neither does it imply a rejection. Something must have aroused Kafka's interest. We are, therefore, left with an impression of ambivalence, a feeling quite often found in Kafka's life and work. On the whole, Kafka, as we would expect from a writer who had just completed his first volume, must have been in a very good mood.

In a note to Max Brod the next day, Kafka referred to the volume of stories, remembering that he was "under the young woman's influence, and it may well be that some silliness resulted" (L, 84). Felice Bauer, it is evident, could exert an influence on a man. Kafka could have established contact with her shortly after their first meeting. He did not do so, possibly due to his ambivalent attitude toward her. But after five weeks of precarious waiting, he contacted her by letter. He did not expect her to have "the remotest recollection" of him (or this is what he wrote) and reintroduced himself by referring to a few details of that evening. He reminded her of a plan to journey together to Palestine the next year ("with the very hand now striking the [typewriter] keys, [I] held your hand, the one which confirmed a promise . . .") (F, 5).

We do not know how serious the Palestine plan was. Felice was a Zionist and Kafka had at least an emotional attachment to the Holy Land. But the fact that she so quickly agreed to accompany Kafka on that trip would indicate that the project was not a realistic one. A point can be made that the plan had a different weight for Kafka than for Felice. In his first letter to her (September 20, 1912), he returned to the plan. "If you still wish to undertake this journey," it would be essential to start discussions on the details at once. They should prepare themselves as thoroughly as possible and try to agree on all preparations.

The letter introduced a moment of doubt that could be raised (by Felice, her family, Kafka's family?) about himself as "traveling companion, guide, encumbrance, tyrant, or whatever else I might turn into." However, nothing could speak against an exchange of letters between the two. Here, too, he added a word of warning: he presented himself as "an erratic letter writer. [. . .] I never expect a letter to be answered by return" and "am never disappointed when it doesn't come." A vivid correspondence ensued; soon it becomes clear that the correspondence was the chief expression of the Kafka–Felice friendship. Alas, Felice's letters were not preserved; all we have from her side are occasional references in Kafka's letters to some of her words.

Two days later Kafka wrote the story "The Judgment" in the course of one night. For the first time he felt satisfied, even overjoyed, with what came out of his pen. He experienced how "everything can be said, how for everything, for the strangest fancies, there waits a great fire in which they perish and rise up again." "Only in this way can writing be done, only with such coherence, with such a complete opening out of the body and the soul" (DI, 276). At a later date he noted that the story came out of him "like a real birth, covered with filth and slime" (DI, 278).

The theme of the story is the abysmal antagonism between father and son and the lack of even an initial understanding between them. It is easy to recognize the biographical background of the story. The end, however, goes beyond the feeling of hatred between Franz and his father. In the story, the father addresses his son, "a devilish human being": "I sentence you now to death by drowning." The son calls out in a low voice, "Dear parents, I have always loved you, all the same," and lets himself drop into the river.

The story appeared in print with the dedication "Für Fräulein Felice B." It is not easy to imagine the negative impression Kafka's tale must have made on Felice. Nor is it easy to understand the impatience with which Kafka expected Felice to appreciate it or, at least, to show *some* form of gratitude. But nothing arrived to please the young writer or simply to acknowledge his efforts.

At mid-December, Kafka sent Felice a copy of the newly published *Meditation*, the collection of short pieces he brought as manuscript to Brod that evening of the first meeting with Felice. He begs her, "Please be kind to my poor book! [. . .] Show the book to as few people as possible, so as to avoid having your mind about me changed. Goodnight, dearest, goodnight" (F, 100).

Silently awaiting Felice's letters, Kafka continued writing his stories. "The Judgment" was followed by "The Stoker" (which was to become Chapter One of *Amerika*) and several chapters to follow "The Stoker." While at work on *Amerika*, he wrote "The Metamorphosis," one of the best known (and least understood) of his short stories.

Kafka's state of mind was not what the reader would expect from a writer happily at work. He wrote to Felice: "Oh, the moods I get into, Fräulein Bauer! A hail of nervousness pours down upon me continuously. What I want one minute I don't want the next. When I have reached the top of the stairs, I still don't know the state I shall be in when I enter the apartment. I have to pile up uncertainties within myself before they turn into a little certainty or a letter. [. . .] My memory is very bad, but even the best of memories could not help me to write down accurately even a short paragraph which I have thought out in advance and tried to memorize." However, a letter from Felice makes him "absurdly happy." He suggests she keep a little diary for him; this "demands less and gives more" (F, 6f.).

Kafka must have concluded that Felice did not like his book. "Why don't you tell me, tell me in two words, that you don't like it!—You wouldn't have to say you don't like it (which probably wouldn't be true anyway), but simply that you can't make head or tail of it. It really is full of hopeless confusion, or rather there are glimpses into endless perplexities, and one has to come very close to see anything at all" (F, 132). In other words, beyond liking or disliking the stories as such, Kafka expected from Felice a measure of acceptance, a going-along irrespective of the goal, a sharing, "for we belong—or so I thought—together." Felice considered Kafka's problem a problem of literature and failed to sense here a problem of life. And although Kafka expected some opinion on the stories as stories, he hoped Felice would find a way from the stories to the writer's very life.

Regardless of Felice's "opinion" on Kafka's work and "no matter how much I find fault with it (only its brevity is perfect)," he feels he must confess, "I am so happy to think that my book is in your possession" (F, 104). He is content that a part of him (the book) is now a part of her (her collection). An erotic undertone is evident. "I am in urgent need of having my lips sealed with kisses," concludes his letter.

In states of confusion it is Felice who helps him; thinking of her brings him peace of mind and healing. "Stay with me entirely, dearest, stay for me as you are." "I am writing to you because I am wholly filled with you and must in some way let it be known to the outside world" (F, 118f.). Returning home one evening, he finds a telegram on the table. "You dearest, compassionate heart, I [. . .] knew at once that it could contain nothing but comfort, and when it turned out to be so, I kissed this alien paper, a long kiss with eyes closed, until this was no longer enough for me, and I pressed it flat against my cheek" (F, 119).

Felice evidently informed Kafka of some of the books she was reading at the time. She could not have anticipated an outbreak of jealousy on Kafka's part. Kafka, who had an overly critical view of contemporary writers but did not care to publicize his assessments, was, in a letter to Felice, quite outspoken. Felice must have mentioned Franz Werfel, Ricarda Huch, Selma Lagerlöf, Jens Peter Jacobsen, Herbert Eulenberg, and others. Kafka, in brushing all of them aside, realized that he was doing them injustice; some may have written decent things, but he wanted to prevent Felice from reading them. She must have expressed her enthusiasm for Eulenberg (while calling him Her*mann*), whose style Kafka considered less than mediocre. "I could hardly bear it, the breathless unclean prose" (F, 129).

Sometime later, Felice mentioned the poet Else Lasker-Schüler. Kafka: "I cannot bear her poems; their emptiness makes me feel nothing but boredom, and their contrived verbosity nothing but antipathy. Her prose I find just as tiresome and for the same reasons; it is the work of an indiscriminate brain twitching in the head of an overwrought city-dweller. [. . .] Yes, she is in a bad way. [. . .] I don't quite know why, but I always imagine her simply as a drunk, dragging herself through the coffeehouses at night. [. . .] Away with you, Lasker-Schüler! Come here, dearest! No one is to be between us, no one around us" (F, 191).

Next to be rejected by Kafka was the successful dramatist Arthur Schnitzler: "I don't like Schnitzler at all, and hardly respect him; no doubt he is capable of certain things, but for me his great plays and his great prose are full of a truly staggering mass of the most sickening drivel. It is impossible to be too hard on him. [. . .] Only when looking at his photograph—that bogus dreaminess, that sentimentality I wouldn't touch even with the tips of my fingers. [. . .] Enough, enough! Let me quickly get rid of Schnitzler who is trying to come between us, like Lasker-Schüler the other day" (F, 193). Felice—alert, openminded, clear-cut, modern—could not possibly follow Kafka's subtle points. She may have (falsely) interpreted these as nothing more than her friend's prickly jealousy.

The literary interlude about contemporary writers was just that: an interlude. What angered Kafka most was that Felice spoke of the writers she mentioned as "poets," forgetting that Kafka was, if anything, a poet. Kafka, the poet, had to understand this and stop complaining. He did.

The warm attitude returned soon and lasted a long while.

"Dearest, my dearest, out of love for you, only out of love, I would like to dance with you; for I now feel that dancing, this embracing and turning at the same time, belongs inseparably to love and is its true and crazy expression" (F, 121). "Tell me you will go on loving me, no matter how I behave go on loving me at any price. [. . .] 'Do you love me, Felice?' The big yeses follow each other into eternity, everything else can be conquered" (F, 122). "If only, instead of writing my novel, I had written to you, as I very much wanted to! I was so eager to start the letter and to prepare for my writing by covering the paper with kisses, because it will be held by you. But now I am tired and dull and more than your kisses I should need that lively look of yours. [. . .] On the other hand I have the opportunity of pulling the whole face toward me by kissing it, which I do, and shall do again just before going to sleep, and shall do again when I wake up. If it is worth mentioning, my lips are entirely yours, I kiss no one else, neither parents, nor sisters, and implacable aunts find a spot only on a reluctant cheek" (F, 124f.). "I have just kissed you, whereupon your smile was a trifle more friendly than before" (F, 125). "But now goodnight, dearest, and a long, calm, confident kiss" (F, 130). "How could I not be well as long as you love me" (F, 131).

"Of the two of us, it is you who are clarity, and it seems to me that all the clarity I possess I learned that August evening from your eyes" (F, 132). "A happy New Year [1913] to my dearest girl; a new year must be a different year, and if the old one has kept us apart, perhaps the new year, with miraculous forces, will throw us together. Throw, throw, New Year!" (F, 135).

Only a few weeks pass, however, before Kafka is unable to sustain his fragile euphoria. "Dearest, take me to you, hold me, don't lose faith; the days cast me back and forth; you must realize that you will never get unadulterated happiness from me; only as much unadulterated suffering as one could wish for, and yet— don't send me away. I am tied to you not by love alone, love would not be much, love begins, loves comes, passes, and comes again; but this need, by which I am utterly chained to your being, this remains. So you too, dearest, must remain" (F, 161).

His poor physical condition became of ever greater concern to Kafka; it affected his writing, his relationship to friends and family. He became ever more sensitive to noise. "I cannot live with people; I absolutely hate all my relatives, not because they are my relatives, not because they are wicked, not because I don't think well of them (which by no means diminishes my 'terrible timidity,' as you suggest), but simply because they are the people with whom I live in close proximity. It is just that I cannot abide communal life. [. . .] I would [. . .] be incomparably happier living in a desert, in a forest, on an island." Kafka goes as far as to doubt whether he is a human being "often—and in my inmost self perhaps all the time" (F, 287).

The writing of the novel *Amerika* had already stopped some time ago. He continues writing to Felice; he calls her "dearest" but only rarely concludes the letter with a kiss or the wish to embrace her. There is an uncanny tiredness throughout. He tries to convince her "of the impossibility of any kind of human relationship," but begs her to take him as he is, "but don't forget, don't forget to throw me out at the right moment!" (F, 216). He admits that his view of the hopelessness of the world is due largely to a distorted judgment which could not change permanently. His feeling for Felice undergoes a severe critique; he questions Felice's love ("You lack true insight into my wretched personality") and suggests that "not for two days could you live beside me" (F, 215). He commiserates with her: "Goodnight, my poor dearest, dream of pleasanter things than of your Franz" (F, 218). And all this a scant six months since their first meeting.

Still, his longing for Felice persists. "If only I could once, Felice—for once would be always—be so close to you that talking and listening would be one: silence" (F, 223). He suggested that they meet in Berlin at Easter, Sunday or Monday (March 23–24, 1913). Felice's response was not really encouraging, but Kafka journeyed to Berlin in the hope of meeting Felice, and also to present himself to Felice's family. He arrived in Berlin on the night of March 22, staying at the Hotel Askanische Hof. The meeting was a very short one; the "lover" left Berlin on March 24. Yet even the brief meeting was of significance to Kafka. "Do you know that now, since my return, you seem even more incomprehensibly miraculous than ever?" writes Kafka (F, 229), and a few days later he quotes from a letter by Felice: "You say I had become indispensable to you? Pray God that this is true, my whole being cries out, and am I to smother that cry with my own hand?" (F, 231). He is driven by a sad premonition: "My one fear [. . .] is that I shall never be able to possess you. [. . .] I would sit beside you and, as has happened, feel the breath and life of your body at my side, yet in reality be further from you than now, here in my room" (F, 233). That Kafka had fears of impotence, or at least of partial impotence, cannot be denied.

Felice must have had an intuition of what was going on in Kafka's heart and must have used the term "estrangement" in her letter. Kafka answered: "I, dearest, become estranged? I who die of longing for you here at my desk?" (F, 234). Yet honesty compels him to tell her that it is his "perpetual concern to free you of me" (F, 243). He suggests that there may well be more suitable men to deserve Felice's hand, and he, Kafka, would be rightfully expelled from her presence, "since I did not hold you by your hands, as one holds one's beloved" (F, 243). He goes so far as to try to persuade Felice that their union could not possibly be successful, since his real interest is writing. "Writing is actually the good part of my nature. If there is anything good about me, it is that" (F, 275). Regardless of her view of his writing now (he has written nothing for five months!), if, later, she did not come to love it, "there would be absolutely nothing for you to hold on to [. . .] and you would be terribly lonely" (F, 275). Thus, it is his attitude to writing that seems to be an obstacle to their marriage. Writing is a part of his nature, and what he needs for his writing is seclusion. And since he can only write in this regular, continuous fashion, he fears the intrusion of even the most intimate friend. How could people come to see them "without having an intolerably disturbing influence" on him, and also on his wife? And he quotes Felice: "Whether you are capable of living in such seclusion, you do not know" (F, 279). Even if she has the courage to give herself to him, does he "have the right to claim you?" he asks himself and Felice (F, 280). These tortuous letters were "becoming intolerable" (F, 281).

On May 11 and 12, 1913, Kafka and Felice met in Berlin; he was introduced to her family. Torn by his closeness to Felice, he writes, "Tell me, do you feel how much I love you?" (F, 257). The emotional state reminded him of his love experiences some seven or eight years ago: "There were girls I fell in love with easily, was gay with, and left with even greater ease, or who left me without causing the slightest pain. [. . .] There may have been one woman I loved enough to feel shaken to my very depths" (F, 259). He will later recall "that sweetness one experiences in a relationship with a woman one loves" (DII, 112); it is this experience he refers to when he says, "I have never yet been intimate with a woman apart from that time in Zuckmantel. [. . .] [She] was a woman, and I was ignorant" (DII, 159).

What moved Kafka to inform Felice of the intimacies of the past, when his intention was not to reject her but to come closer to her? He does not tell. Was it his intention to show Felice that (though some years ago) he was desirable enough to attract the attention of women? There is no doubt that he did not want to lose Felice. "The more I came to know you, the more I loved you; the

Kafka and his fiancée, Felice Bauer, 1917

more you came to know me, the more insufferable you thought me" (F, 263). Perhaps he wanted to allude to the fact that (though in the past) women saw in him what Felice failed to recognize: a lover.

The lover found the present situation intolerable and let out a cry of despair: "I cannot go on living in this way." He asked her not to write him anymore, as he will not write to her, though he would respond to "the faintest but genuine appeal." As it is today, "you don't want me, you don't want me, nothing could be more obvious" (F, 263).

Three days later, he retracts this final notice: "After all, we do belong together" though there is no doubt that "we are immensely different," Felice being healthy in every sense of the word and thus "calm in your innermost being," whereas he, Kafka, is ill "perhaps not so much in the generally accepted sense, but consequently in the worst possible sense of the word, hence I am restive, absent-minded, listless." Due to these differences, "I make you suffer and yet, as you say, you are quite satisfied with me, and you make me suffer." This not really promising letter concludes: "Deep within me is nothing but love for you, yet bitterness still obtrudes" (F, 264f.).

There was still a good measure of love in Kafka to want to continue this epistolary affair. On June 7 he wrote: "Meanwhile I must be happy that these lips, which in truth, today and always, I dare and can kiss only from afar, have still got some kind words for me" (F, 266). Felice must have sensed that behind Kafka's harsh self-criticism and self-doubts hid a person of utter honesty and goodness of heart. She must have read the positive element in a letter of June 15: "What makes me persecute you? [. . .] On the pretext of wanting to free you of me, I force myself upon you. [. . .] I experience not only my own suffering, but even more that which I inflict upon you" (F, 269).

Kafka must have realized that Felice's peculiarities and her inability to adjust "her schedule" to his were but surface phenomena. So, after letting her consider the changes that marriage would bring about for both (Kafka losing his loneliness; Felice her Berlin, girl friends, small pleasures of life, the prospect of marrying a decent, healthy man), he asks her (in writing, of course): "Will you consider whether you wish to be my wife? Will you do that?" (F,270).

Both Felice and Kafka knew that their married life would be a difficult one; that what is essential to marriage is personal harmony, far deeper than that of opinions; that personal proximity would present problems. Felice agreed—we don't know under what conditions. Neither do we know with what reservations, spoken or unspoken.

We do know that soon after the engagement was agreed upon, the old apprehensions came back to plague the young couple. Would Kafka, the silent, lonely, unwell, tormented writer, be able to do justice to the down-to-earth, healthy, energetic woman with a basically bourgeois taste? Kafka's mother, wishing to know more about Felice and her family, turned to a Berlin detective agency for information, an act deeply offensive to Felice. The Bauers also wished to get parallel information on the Kafkas. They withdrew the order, but the entire affair introduced a sour note into the relationship between the two families (F, 282ff.). Kafka tried to assure Felice that the "inquiries" were of no significance, "that I love you as much as I have any power to love, and that I wish to serve you and must serve you, as long as I live" (F, 288). And: "God, it really is about time to ease the pressure, and there surely isn't a girl who has been loved as I love you, and been tortured as I find it necessary to torture you" (F, 289). "We belong together and shall be together" (F, 291).

However, looking ahead, Kafka does not envisage a life of love and harmony. "I am absurdly afraid of our future and of the unhappiness which, through my fault and temperament, could develop from our life together" (F, 293). And, considering Felice: "Somehow you still seem to me not wholly committed" (F, 294). The meeting with Felice's parents was not successful; Felice's mother was dressed all in black, obviously disapproving, reproachful, stiff. Yet that should not disturb Kafka's relationship with Felice. "I dream about you," writes Kafka, "almost every night, such is my need to be near you" (F, 295). But perhaps you, Felice, "love me only on account of some distant memory. Miserable, uncontrollable begging" (F, 297).

Though doubts remained, so did Kafka's strong attachment. "I feel my ties with you to be immensely powerful." He is grateful to her for everything, "continually when contemplating your picture" (F, 301).

However, he did not succeed in convincing Felice of the seriousness of his prime concern: his writing. She consulted a graphologist. The specialist found the writer to be "very determined in his behavior, extremely sensual, and having artistic interests." The latter "interpretation" especially annoyed Kafka: "I have no artistic interests, but am made of literature, I am nothing else, and cannot be anything else" (F, 304). Felice should have known this. Alas, she did not.

Sadly realizing their futility, Kafka asked her to reduce the frequency of her letters (which in the past had meant so very much to him). He tries with all his strength of persuasion to impress upon her that what awaits her is not the life of a happy couple, "but a monastic life at the side of a man who is peevish, miserable, silent" (F, 308), a life in which, as a married woman, she "will find loneliness harder to bear than you can possibly imagine now from afar" (F, 309). He signs this letter as a man "blinded by love as I was and am." Another conclusion of a letter: "Allow me—and this is something I have not dared to imagine for a long time—allow me to give you a long, calm kiss, as calm as possible" (F, 311). He calls her his guardian angel," and every day I am more convinced that you are" though, he says, he has been without a guardian angel for a long time (F, 312).

He was more practical in writing to her father at the end of August. He stresses the differences between the two: she, Felice, is healthy, self-confident, and should be surrounded by healthy, lively people, while he, Kafka, is deeply devoted to literature, taciturn, unsociable, morose, selfish, a hypochondriac, and actually in poor health—things Kafka had many times written to his beloved without forcing a decision upon her. "I love her too much, and she cannot see me as I am" (F, 313). Felice did not give her father the letter. Kafka writes to Felice: "We shall have to part" (F, 320).

In the first days of September, Kafka had started on a trip that took him to Vienna (where he attended a Zionist Congress), Triest, Venice, Verona, and Lake Garda. At Riva, he entered a sanatorium for a few days' rest.

A previously mentioned erotic experience during his stay in Riva was deeply significant to Kafka, and he felt he should entrust it to Felice. He "fell in love" with a Swiss girl who was about eighteen years old. "Still immature but remarkable and despite her illness a real person with great depth." Both knew that they did not really belong together, "and that once the ten days available to us had expired everything would have to end, and that no letters would be exchanged. Nevertheless, we meant a great deal to each other." When we said goodbye, he had to see to it that she did not break into tears in front of everyone. "I felt much the same." Kafka promised not to tell the story and not to reveal her name, beyond her initials, G.W., to anyone. "With my departure it was all over" (F, 335).

All this Kafka writes to Felice. Did he think the experience would make his feelings about Felice clearer to him? The opposite was the case. Returning to Prague, he found himself "completely out of touch" with Felice, and "lost more and more courage" (F, 335). He hoped a meeting in Berlin in December might help him arrive at a decision.

In his diaries, Kafka noted that the stay in Riva was very important to him. "For the first time I understood a Christian girl and lived almost entirely within the sphere of her influence" (DI, 301). Later, looking back on his intimate encounters, he wrote, "With F[elice] I never experienced (except in letters) that sweetness one experiences in a relationship with a woman one loves, such as I had in Zuckmantel and Riva" (DII, 112). He had "really come to the end" (F, 321). Felice was ready to give at least a try to their relationship, fragile as it had now become. In October 1913, unable to think of a better solution, she decided to send her friend Grete Bloch to Prague, to mediate between Kafka, who had become silent, and herself.

Grete Bloch, then twenty-one years old, was an executive secretary in a Berlin business firm, known for her intelligence, efficiency, cleverness, and a sense for beauty and order. A meeting was arranged, and Kafka prayed, "Let heaven look upon us with understanding" (F, 325), which indicates that he had no hope for a positive outcome of the talks.

The next step was an unexpected one—or, perhaps, knowing Kafka, not unexpected at all. Though getting to know Grete Bloch but slightly, he fell in love with her. In an early letter to her (November 10, 1913), he mentions by the way that he is "sorry for all girls," "perhaps [. . .] on account of the transformation into women which they have to undergo" (F, 327). This remark could be taken as the key to Kafka's attitude to the opposite sex. He was not really attracted to mature women, though he knew that marriage to a very young girl was frowned upon by society. In becoming or (as he says) being transformed into women, they lose the precious quality of being young, a quality so deeply attractive to

Kafka. That would explain the immediate closeness to the shopgirl long ago, the Swiss girl G.W., and others, and the ambivalence toward Felice.

When Grete Bloch arrived in Prague, Kafka was surprised to meet "a slim, young, undoubtedly rather unusual girl" (F, 327), who immediately captivated him, while her report, in great detail, of Felice's trouble with her teeth made a bad impression on him; he considered dental trouble "among the most repulsive ailments" and a mark of an older woman. (Later, he was told of Felice's gold-capped teeth, which required an emotional adjustment on Kafka's part.) A few days later he wrote to Grete that, upon receiving her letter, he wanted to "do something that would be equivalent to kissing your hand" (F, 329).

Nevertheless, there developed a renewal of the Kafka–Felice friendship and a wish to get married. "Marriage is the only means whereby the relationship between us—so very necessary to me—can be maintained" (F, 337). However, Felice told Kafka he should "live more in the real world," should take things as he finds them, which, Kafka says, must imply that "you no longer want me" (F, 338). Still, he tells Grete Bloch in January 1914, "I have renewed my request for her hand and have received no, or virtually no, reply. [. . .] I don't understand it" (F, 339).

But that was not the end. Kafka to Felice: "In spite of everything [. . .], when your postcard arrived today, it was again as on the first day. [. . .] At least you show yourself to me, you wish to have something to do with me after all. [. . .] I felt faint with joy when I read it" (F, 345). "Don't withdraw the hand you now hold out to me, however weakly. Let me hold on to it, as you once allowed me to" (F, 346).

Kafka gives a summary report to Grete Bloch: "F. quite likes me, but in her opinion this is not enough for marriage; she has insurmountable fears about a joint future; she might not be able to put up with my idiosyncrasies; she might not be able to forego Berlin;

she is afraid of having to dispense with nice clothes, of traveling
third class, sitting in cheaper seats in the theater [. . .], etc. On
the other hand she is friendly toward me [. . .]; in the streets we
walk arm in arm like the happiest of engaged couples," etc. (F,
353). A prudent friend or marriage counselor would no doubt have
advised the couple not to plan marriage; their differences were too
considerable and of long standing. No change of attitudes and
direction could be expected—better to break off now than after
some sorry experiences that will surely occur. The fact that Felice
wanted to keep Kafka's letters and photographs was not sufficient
ground to be hopeful of the future.

What remained was Kafka's strong attachment to Grete. A letter
to her in March concludes: "Farewell, and please go on being a
good friend to your (how shall I put it) Franz K." (F, 356). And,
two days later: "Do come, do come if it is at all possible" (F, 356).
(The meeting did not come about.) Kafka's friendship with Grete
was not unknown to his friends. One of them, Dr. Ernst Weiss, is
quoted as saying: " 'Fr. Bloch seems to mean a great deal to you.' I
could only answer in the affirmative" (F, 358).

In a letter to Wolfgang Alexander Schocken, a family friend,
dated April 21, 1940, Grete revealed that she was the mother of a
son conceived by Kafka in 1914. According to her version, the
child was put in the care of foster parents in Munich and died in
1921, at about seven years of age. Kafka was never told of the
matter. Wolfgang Schocken accepts the story, while some Kafka
experts (e.g., Erich Heller [F, 323f.]) reject it. If true, it would
constitute a further irony in Kafka's life that the man who at times
longed for children and at other times doubted whether he could
be a father should have been kept in ignorance of his son.

We ask again: And Felice? "To me the situation with F. is so
unclear, or rather, somewhere so deep down that my eyes can

hardly reach it, so terribly clear that with every word I say it becomes even more obscure, more turbid, more agonizing" (F, 360).

Kafka was longing to meet Grete at a neutral place, "somewhere halfway one Saturday evening and spend Sunday together. Would you like that? I would love it" (F, 360). At about the same time, Kafka wrote to Felice that he was most anxious to meet her "in order to get things as clear and to be as free as possible to decide"; he suggested a date for a meeting in Berlin (F, 365). The issue at hand "has to be brought to an end, good or bad" (F, 367). One of the difficulties was that Kafka, as reported by Felice, had said he was content with the love she had for him, which implied (in Kafka's view) that she was prepared to sacrifice herself, realizing that he could not do without her. "Why do you want to sacrifice yourself, why? Don't keep asking whether I want you!" (F, 369).

Kafka considered this statement to be ("probably") the last one. At the time, he accepted the fact that the differences between the two were really serious. Yet they did not imply a rejection of Felice. In a letter to Grete Bloch, Kafka called Grete "the best, kindest, and sweetest creature," adding: "and so is F. [. . .]; this will remain my opinion forever and I shall never abandon it. [. . .] She just can't help behaving like this toward me and we must resign ourselves to it. Perhaps the force that ties me to her and that which keeps her away from me are one and the same. There is really nothing to be done" (F, 371). Kafka's reference to a force, at one and the same time positive and negative, demonstrates a keen psychological insight. We shall see whether or not he was able to translate this insight into action.

The ambiguous relationship continues. Kafka assures Felice: "I love you, F., to the limits of my strength, in this respect you can trust me entirely. But for the rest, F., I do not know myself completely. Surprises and disappointments about myself [. . .] will be mine alone; I shall use all my strength to see that none but the pleasant, the pleasantest surprises of my nature will touch you" (F, 372). Felice asked whether it was possible for him to take her as though nothing had happened. Kafka answers that "it is not possible. But what is possible, and in fact necessary, is for me to take you with all that has happened, and to hold on to you to the point of delirium" (F, 373). To Grete Bloch, Kafka wrote that the fresh encounter with Felice "may be a new and good beginning" (F, 374). There is no doubt that both sides tried hard to reach an agreeable outcome of the problem that bothered both, each from a different angle. Kafka sadly saw that Felice had not changed; "F. never tires of keeping me waiting," he wrote to Grete Bloch (F, 374).

Keeping the man waiting was a chief motive in this strange love affair. Grete Bloch was more definite and alert in her handling of Kafka.

Kafka met Felice at Easter in Berlin, and the unofficial engagement took place there on April 12–13, 1914.

The engagement did not bring to an end the division in Kafka's heart. He complained that he and Felice were never alone and that he could never draw comfort from her in a kiss; he could have given her the opportunity, "yet did not do so." The rights bestowed on him as fiancé "are repellent to me and perfectly useless"(F, 384)—not a very passionate statement by one newly engaged. On the very same day he wrote to Grete Bloch, who had sent a telegram of congratulations: "It would be nicer if instead of the telegram I were holding your hand" (F, 385).

It is difficult, if not impossible, to guess what was in Felice's mind these weeks after the engagement. Kafka quotes one of her letters: "Am I aware of the fact that I am entirely yours?" It sounds almost like a rejection of the question when he replies: "I did not have to become aware of that, I have known it for 18 months"—a reference to the first meeting. "My awareness could not be established more firmly. [. . .] You, F., don't quite realize how completely and in how special a fashion I belong to you." Yet Kafka knew well that much remained to be done for Felice and himself to make this "the most united of couples." "If only we had reached that point!" he adds in that letter (F, 391). Despite lingering doubts, Kafka trusts in that union; "no rabbinical blessing could bring you closer" (F, 392). He confesses—not for the first time—that he has become "more and more taciturn, more and more unsociable" and beset by "a feeling of discomfort in the presence of people, an inability to establish complete, lasting relationships." In contrast to this failing, nothing separates him from Felice, "now that I have you" (F, 393). At the same time (precisely one day later), he explained to Grete that his recent letter, which Grete apparently misunderstood, was "meant to be a grasping and clasping of your hand [. . .] and you know it" (F, 394). Contrast this grasping of Grete's hand with the conclusion of a letter to Felice: "Allow me at least to kiss your hand" (F, 396).

On a planned journey with Grete: "I do look forward to sitting opposite you in the compartment [. . .], just to sit there, nodding, shaking my head, squeezing your hand properly by way of greeting, and altogether being at ease. Lovely journey!" (F, 397). Looking forward to his marriage, Kafka writes to Grete that he and Felice have decided that "you are to come and live with us for some time—and from the very beginning. [. . .] We shall lead a pleasant life and, in order to test me, you shall hold my hand and I, in order to thank you, must be allowed to hold yours" (F, 403). Grete accepted the invitation.

At the end of May 1914, Kafka traveled with his father to Berlin to celebrate the official engagement; his mother and his sister Ottla were in Berlin already. The celebration (June 1) took place at the Bauer home; Grete Bloch attended. To her, Kafka wrote: "You cannot be fully aware of what you mean to me," concluding the short note with: "And now I merely kiss your dear hand" (F, 419).

Grete Bloch
Photograph courtesy of Klaus Wagenbach

The engagement was a torment, both for Kafka and for Felice: the many unfamiliar faces, the artificial cordiality, the forced behavior of the couple. Kafka was in a terrible mood. In his diaries he noted: "Was tied hand and foot like a criminal. Had they set me down in a corner bound in real chains, placed policemen in front of me and let me look on simply like that, it could not have been worse. And that was my engagement. [. . .] Felice suffered the most" (DII, 42). He tells Grete—for the time being she is the only one to be told—that he really does not know how, being as he is, he can assume the responsibility of marriage (F, 420).

Unfortunately, the extant biographical material is not sufficient for an understanding of this decisive chapter in Kafka's life. Grete must have envied Felice, and Kafka must have been unable to be fair to the two women, especially since his innermost attachment was with Grete and it was her love he was ardently seeking. It was of no help that at this point the parents (Kafka's and Felice's) were emotionally involved in the affairs of their children. Felice was an independent person and Kafka one of the most private individuals possible. The very fact of the parents' active interest was a negative one. The families decided to come together to discuss the situation, in the hope of resolving what disturbed the relationship between the engaged couple. The meeting took place July 12 at the Hotel Askanische Hof in Berlin. In addition to Kafka and Felice, those present were Grete Bloch, Erna Bauer (Felice's sister), and Kafka's friend Ernst Weiss. We are not informed of the details of the discussion, but we do know that Grete, representing Felice, led the conversation, and that Kafka was completely silent; he neither accused anyone nor defended himself. Kafka called the meeting "the tribunal in the hotel." Felice "patted her hair with her hand, wiped her nose, yawned" (DII, 65). "I realized that all was lost. [. . .] I loved you then as I do now; I knew that though innocent, you had been made to suffer for two years as even the guilty ought not to suffer; but I also realized that you could not understand my position" (F, 437). Erna Bauer still hoped it would end well, or acted as if she did. She "consoled me, though I wasn't sad; that is, my sadness has to do only with myself, but as such it is inconsolable" (DII, 66).

That evening Kafka sat alone on a bench on Unter den Linden. He recalled the years of his and Felice's friendship, their "love," and their decision to marry and establish a home (DII, 65f). He recalled his attempts to make Felice aware of the "immense power my work has over me," a matter she "did appreciate [. . .], but by no means fully." She was, as he informs her, both "the greatest friend [and] the greatest enemy of my work." He reminded her of his unusual working schedule: on the average he sat at his desk until 5:00 in the morning, then slept. This kind of life was not acceptable to a woman like Felice; and though she never said "no" in reply to the question of his way of life, her "yes" "never encompassed the entire question"—a sense of dislike remained. Another point of difference between the two was the apartment: Felice's wish for a bourgeois home actually frightened Kafka. Kafka outlined these reflections in a long letter that later encompassed over five printed pages (F, 436–41).

Who was the judge at the tribunal in Berlin? Apparently Grete Bloch. But, Kafka noted, it was true that "you sat in judgment over me—it was horrible for you, for me, for everyone—but it only appeared to be so; in fact I was sitting in your place, which to this day I have not left" (F, 436).

Though the engagement had come to an end, the relationship between Kafka and Felice continued. The two met in Bodenbach, formerly a border town between Bohemia and Germany (January 23–24, 1915). Erna's prediction seemed to come true. It was Kafka who felt that the abrupt end did not do justice to Felice, though "it is impossible for us ever to unite." Thus, he held out hope to her again, stupidly, for every day made him older and crustier. His old headaches returned when he tried "to comprehend that she is suffering and is at the same time calm and gay. We shouldn't torment each other again by a lot of writing" (DII, 111).

The memory of past differences came alive. Especially annoying to Kafka was Felice's habit (it was more than habit) of setting his watch—which for the past three months had been an hour and a half fast—right to the minute. After all, he lived either behind the times (often in ages past, or beyond time) or as a critical proclaimer of things to occur; his watch could not possibly indicate "the right time" (DII, 111). How could Felice, a businesswoman in a high position, understand this?

The choice of furniture for their future home created disagreements. Felice spoke of a "personal touch" in the furnishings; Kafka wanted but the barest minimum of objects in the home. Felice "asks almost no questions about my work and has no apparent understanding of it" (DII, 112). Felice's lack of literary interest was obvious to Kafka from the very beginning; now, and looking back, this failing grew in proportion. Possibly as a last attempt to test her interests, Kafka read to her aloud; the listener lay on the sofa with closed eyes (open eyes would have demonstrated her boredom) and made a lukewarm request to be permitted to take a manuscript along to copy it. Kafka was fair enough to admit that the "doorkeeper story" ("Before the Law") elicited "greater attention and good observation." "The significance of the story dawned upon me for the first time; she grasped it rightly too" (DII, 112). Yet this was not enough. "All of it [was] senseless; after all, she has no sense of guilt" (DII, 113).

What mattered most and what drove him to make a final decision was the serious nature of his work. "Thus, though fundamentally it [my work] loved you beyond measure, equally it had to resist you with all its might for the sake of self-preservation" (F, 437). Dr. Ernst Weiss, who disliked Felice, "tries to convince [Kafka] that F. deserves to be hated, F. tries to convince me that

W. deserves to be hated. I believe them both and love them both,
or try to" (DII, 113). He turns to Felice: "Tell me candidly, do you
think there is a future for us together in Prague" (F, 447)—or any
other place?

Kafka tried to conceal from Felice the deep conflict in which he
found himself. He advised her that "the only thing that has
happened is that my letters have become less frequent and different," since the more frequent and different letters which he used
to write led to naught. "We must start afresh" (F, 453).

Nevertheless, the ambiguity prevailed. "Yes" and "no" were
equally forceful. At times he "had been longing for her unbear-
ably," in a state of passion. Yet, reflecting on other people's
relationship to him, Kafka ranks Felice last: "Ottla understands
many things, even a great many; Max, Felix, many things; others,
like E[rnst], understand only details, but with dreadful intensity;
F[elice] in all likelihood understands nothing, which, because of
our undeniable inner relationship, places her in a very special
position." He wished for someone possessed of such understanding, "a wife perhaps [which] would mean to have support from
every side, to have God" (DII, 126). So "no," she has no understanding, but "yes," there is an inner relationship. Once this
ambiguity is accepted, there is nothing to prevent Kafka, Felice,
Grete Bloch, and Felice's sister Erna from spending the spring
vacation (May 23–24, 1915) together in Bohemian Switzerland.

Another woman that attracted Kafka's attention at the time was
Fanny Reis, a student of Max Brod's in the school for Jewish
refugees. The diaries note briefly: "Was a long time with Miss R. in
the lobby of the hotel yesterday"(DII, 140). Somewhat later:
"Walks with Miss R. With her at *Er und seine Schwester* [by
Bernhard Buchbinder], played by Girardi" (DII, 140).

Girls continue to play a central role. He gives an account of the
girls he has been in a "muddle" with, "in spite of all my headaches,

insomnia, gray hair, despair. [. . .] There have been at least six since the summer. I can't resist, my tongue is fairly torn from my mouth if I don't give in and admire anyone who is admirable and love her until admiration is exhausted. With all six my guilt is almost wholly inward" (DII, 154f.).

The intimacy that marked the early period of Kafka's friendship with Felice was no longer felt in the rare communications. Rare was a marginal line in a letter of late May: "A kiss upon the wide soft hand in its delicate glove" (F, 455). More and more Kafka's misery became the main theme of his letters. What was his principal disease? "Impatience or patience, I am not quite sure which" (F, 456). He considers the present suffering not to be the worst thing. The worst is that time passes, that this suffering makes him more wretched, and prospects for the future become increasingly more dismal. "For weeks on end sleep and delirium are indistinguishable." He remembers their meeting in Bodenbach, where he felt that "F. is here—she is mine—for 2 whole days— what bliss!" which bliss was followed by an unsuccessful trip to Karlsbad and "the truly horrible journey to Aussig" (F, 457). He complained about stabbing pains in his head, but as long as they go no deeper he is thankful. Felice came back to her suggestion to meet in some neutral place. Kafka replied that they had suffered enough from such temporary expedients. "I could bring you nothing but disappointments, monster of insomnia and headaches that I am" (F, 459). He realizes—or pretends to realize—that he has no right to Felice. Under the circumstances, silence is more desirable than the kind of writing he can offer Felice. For now all he could give is a record of despair. "For I am desperate, like a caged rat, insomnia and headaches tearing at me; how I get through the days is quite beyond description" (F, 462).

In a postscript to the letter of March 1916 quoted above, he tries to reduce and correct its severity. He fails completely when he says that he is "hemmed in by ghosts. [. . .] Day and night they cling to me; if only I were free it would be my supreme delight to chase them at my will, but as it is, they gradually do me in. As long as I am not free I don't wish to be seen, and I don't wish to see you" (F, 463). Felice, apparently, had suspected Kafka had other reasons for his refusal to see her: "How utterly wrong you are, how sadly wrong, if you seek other explanations."

Kafka overcame his ills enough to go on an official trip to Marienbad in mid-May 1916. But the "ghosts" did not leave him. "There are ghosts that haunt one in company and those that haunt one in solitude" (F, 467). Later, on July 2, he goes on vacation in Marienbad, where he is joined by Felice. "May we be granted a happy reunion" (F, 472). The first night left both unhappy; the following days were more satisfactory. They had adjoining rooms, with keys on either side.

A note in the diaries: "The hardships of living together. Forced upon us by strangeness, pity, lust, cowardice, vanity, and only deep down, perhaps, a thin little stream worthy of the name of love, impossible to seek out, flashing once in the moment of a moment" (DII, 157).

The headaches continue to plague Kafka, in addition to bad, sleepless nights. He cannot think of an immediate cause, for he is calm and happy with regard to Felice. He wonders whether they are the aftermath of the good time, or eternal companions of his life. He does not rule out the fact that he has been dissipating his energies the past four years—the period of his friendship with Felice. It comes to his mind that his torment is but retribution (F, 475f). In his despair he turns back to Felice: "Your influence over me, Felice, is great and good, and on the strength of the days we have spent together [. . .] I believe you will make excellent use of it" (F, 476). And, though often he evaded meeting her, now he suggests that they meet again soon, for "I try to reach out for the peace I find with you" (F, 477). Four days after his return, he still feels the aftereffects of "that inner and outer calm" which with "your help [. . .] was granted to me in Marienbad" (F, 480). Soon, however, the old ills come to the fore: headaches, nightmares, restless nights; he hopes a little traveling will help "to mend my disintegrating head." He rarely sleeps more than an hour, goes back to sleep, but again for no longer.

Felice fell back into the habit of writing inconsequential letters, no more than alluding to what really concerned her. Kafka encouraged her to be more explicit, more direct. "Being together, one can be silent; true, this shortens life, but then life on average is long. On the other hand, being so far apart, one should take every opportunity to speak frankly" (F, 488).

What, in the last analysis, led Felice and Kafka to the decision to get married we don't know.

Dora Dymant, to whom Kafka later became engaged, offered one assessment: "In the hope that it would enable him to lead the kind of life he wanted, Kafka established a concrete—but by no means bourgeois—relationship to his home, to his family, and to money. I mention this because I remember how quietly and objectively he spoke to me about his former fiancée. She was a splendid girl, but completely bourgeois in outlook. Kafka felt that by marrying her he would have been marrying the whole deceitful world in which she moved; and he also feared that he would have had no time to come to terms with middle-class life. That was one of the principal reasons for his engagement. The other was curiosity. He wanted to get to know everything, and to get to know it in personal terms" (Der Monat I [1949]).

In any case, on August 19, 1916, Kafka notified Felice that "as for our union, it is certain, as certain as human beings can be; the exact time is only relatively certain, and the details of our life together in days to come [. . .] we must leave to the future" (F, 490).

Kafka prays: "Have mercy on me, I am sinful in every nook and cranny of my being. But my gifts were not entirely contemptible; I had some small talents, squandered them, unadvised creature that I was, am now near my end just at a time when outwardly everything might at last turn out well for me. Don't thrust me in among the lost. I know it is my ridiculous love of self that speaks here, ridiculous whether looked at from a distance or close at hand; but, as I am alive, I also have life's love of self, and if life is not ridiculous its necessary manifestations can't be either.—Poor dialectic!" (DII, 161).

"Don't thrust me in among the lost" has the ring of an authentic prayer; it reminds one of the Psalm passage (51:13) "Cast me not away from Thy presence." It is solemnly recited on the Days of Awe, and possibly Kafka recalled the line. Kafka's prayer is followed by the sad cognition: "If I am condemned, then I am not only condemned to die, but also condemned to struggle till I die." A strange premonition in the mouth of a man about to get married. Or is it possible that marriage, suffering, death formed a union in the mind of Kafka, a union to the exclusion of love?

Dr. Siegfried Lehmann (1892–1958), a leading figure in Jewish education in Berlin, later in Israel, founded the Jewish People's Home in Berlin. The Home (Jüdische Volksheim), which employed volunteers ("helpers"), concentrated on the cultural advancement of youth, especially Jewish refugee children from Eastern Europe. Kafka strongly advised Felice to participate in the Home's work. "What matters to me (as it will to you) is not so much Zionism as the thing in itself, and what it may lead to" (F, 481). The modern, humanistic, educational outlook of the Home attracted the non-Zionist Kafka. "Put yourself at [Dr. Lehmann's] disposal" (F, 481).

The suggestion appealed to Felice, who had a strong interest in children, especially those who had lost parents and relatives in the war. "I am absolutely delighted that you are at last in touch with the Home," Kafka writes her in August (F, 489). "Very pleased, Felice, I am very pleased with you" (F, 492). From now on, the

Home becomes a central subject in Kafka's letters to Felice. He advises her, "You need have no qualms about the Jewish Home as regards Zionism, with which you are not sufficiently familiar. Through the Jewish Home other forces, much nearer to my heart, are set in motion and take effect. Zionism, accessible to most Jews of today, at least in its outer fringes, is but an entrance to something far more important" (F, 482). And, a few weeks later: "That you have at last got together, you and the Home, is certainly the most important thing; everything else—being a good, indeed the very best thing that could happen—will solve itself. [. . .] The main thing is the human element, only the human element. I would very much like to hear more about this" (F, 498).

Kafka expects the Home to bring about radical changes in the life of the typical Berlin Jewish young lady. "Only the reality of the Home can teach you anything of importance—any reality, however small. Don't be prejudiced in favor or against, nor let the thought of me affect your open mind. You will see those in need of help, and opportunities of giving help judiciously, and in yourself the power to help—so help. It is very simple, yet more profound than any fundamental ideas. Everything else you ask about will, if you go through with it, follow quite naturally from this one simple fact." Kafka realizes that this work removes her to some extent from him, but "only to some extent." "On the whole I can think of no closer spiritual bond between us than that created by this work" (F, 500).

Between the lines one reads Kafka's wish to give Felice some intellectual grounding outside her business duties and thus free himself from the obligation of caring for her. The style of these letters is correct, objective, instructive, if you will. What is missing is love. "I have deliberately not touched upon that which concerns us and our relationship; on this subject let us be silent" (F, 498). He goes on to hope that Grete Bloch will attach herself to the Home.

Kafka was satisfied with the Home's influence on Felice. "The

Home is turning into a fine meeting place, quite apart from its main purpose. I am delighted to commit you to the care of these people" (F, 511). By December, something must have happened to upset Felice, for Kafka writes, "And the Home? Doesn't it hold your interest, give you strength?" (F, 535). The answer, if there was any, was No.

The conditions in Kafka's home continued to be oppressive for the overly sensitive poet. "I have an infinite longing for independence, self-reliance, freedom in all directions." He finds himself "in the midst of frenzied family life" (F, 524f). Yet he knows well that he is his parents' progeny, bound to them and to his sisters by blood. But he hates "the sight of the [parental] double bed, of sheets that have been slept in; nightshirts carefully laid out can bring me to the point of retching, can turn my stomach inside out; it is as though my birth had not been final, as though from this fusty life I keep being born again and again in this fusty room; as though I had to return there for confirmation, being—if not quite, at least in part—indissolubly connected with these distasteful things" (F, 525). All this unpleasantness is counterbalanced by the rational knowledge that they are his parents, "essential, strength-giving elements of my own self." Often he thinks his sister Ottla would be the kind of mother he should like in the background: "pure, truthful, honest, consistent—with humility and pride [. . .], devotion and self-reliance." But parents are what they are, he cannot rebel against the laws of nature without going mad. "So again there is hatred, and almost nothing but hatred." Then, thinking of Felice: "But you belong to me, I have made you mine; I do not believe that the battle for any woman in any fairy tale has been fought harder and more desperately than the battle for you within myself—from the beginning, over and over again, and perhaps forever. So you belong to me." Now he closes his letters with "Dearest, accept me as I am" (F, 520) and "Kind regards, dearest and best one" (F, 517).

Kafka wrote to Felice about some of the most essential problems of living together on postcards, which he often used instead of letters. From these notes we learn that Felice had, quite casually, accused Kafka of selfishness, "with the ever-present threat of it continuing indefinitely." This affected Kafka deeply—because the accusation was just. "What is unjust is that it should be you, you of all people, who accuse me, thereby denying [. . .] my right to this kind of selfishness. [. . .] My sense of guilt is strong enough at any time, it doesn't need feeding from outside; my constitution, on the other hand, is not strong enough to gulp down this kind of food very often" (F, 534).

Kafka, a most compassionate and caring person, became selfish and intolerant with what concerned his work. He knew no pity when he suspected that his way of doing things (in this case, his writing) might be disturbed. He could have realized that this demanded a lot of consideration from his fellow man and especially from his family; he could have understood that such working conditions were not readily available. Instead, he risked his marriage and his friendship with Felice. His immediate family remained loyal to him but knew that not much of filial love was to be expected in return.

There are no diary entries from October 20, 1916, to April 6, 1917. A copy of a letter to Felice from the end of December 1916 to the beginning of January 1917 describes in detail the engaged couple's search for housing (F, 540ff.). The wedding was scheduled for anytime after the end of the war. Kafka was looking for a very quiet place; he was accompanied by Ottla. Felice hoped for as much comfort as possible. Both conditions were difficult to combine. The quiet apartments were not comfortable, the comfortable ones were not quiet.

At the beginning of July 1917, Felice came to Prague to celebrate their second engagement. It is not apparent what moved Kafka to renew his relationship with Felice, nor is Felice's trend of thought clear. Perhaps a decision, however fragile, was preferable to no decision. The couple made a formal visit to Max Brod (remembering that it was in Brod's home that they met). They traveled to Arad, Hungary, to visit Felice's sister; in Budapest, Kafka met with the actor Yitzhak Levy, with whom he had been friendly when the Yiddish theater played in Prague. In mid-July Kafka returned to Prague—alone.

On September 9, Kafka informed Felice that four weeks previously, one early morning, he had suffered a severe hemorrhage of the lung. The next day he went to see a doctor and, later, a specialist. The verdict was tuberculosis in both lungs. He was not surprised. "For years my insomnia and headaches have invited a serious illness, and ultimately my maltreated blood had to burst forth." He even feels a certain relief; his "headaches seem to have been washed away with the flow of blood" (F, 543). He decides to take leave from his job and retire to his sister in Zürau for at least three months.

From Zürau he writes Felice a letter of confession. "I am a mendacious creature; for me it is the only way to maintain an even keel, my boat is fragile. When I examine my ultimate aim it shows that I do not actually strive to be good. [. . .] I strive [. . .] to become so pleasing that in the end I might openly act out my inherent baseness before the eyes of the world without forfeiting its love—the only sinner not to be roasted" (F, 545).

Did Kafka expect to discourage Felice from giving further thought to marriage? The letter uses the phrase I "would at last be allowed to have you," but the context does not allow this interpretation of the complex situation. For he continues: "Secretly I don't believe this illness to be tuberculosis [. . .] but rather a sign of my general bankruptcy" (F, 545). He concludes by telling Felice a secret which at the moment he does not believe himself—"although the distant darkness that falls about me at each attempt

Kafka, 1917

to work, or think, might possibly convince me"—but which is "bound to be true." The secret: "I will never be well again" (F, 546). In the last extant letter from October 16, 1917, Kafka mentions that he had asked his friends Max Brod, Felix Weltsch, and Oskar Baum not to come and see him (F, 547). The idea was to discourage Felice, too, from visiting.

Now Kafka informed Felice clearly that he wanted a complete separation from her. Both spent the evening (December 25) at the Brods'. Brod noted in his diary: "Both unhappy; don't talk." According to Brod, Kafka said: "What I have to do, I can do only alone. Become clear about the ultimate things. The Western Jew is not clear about them, and therefore has no right to marry. There are no marriages for them. Unless he is the kind that is not interested in such things—businessmen for example." The next morning Kafka came to Brod's office. "He had just been to the station to see F. off. His face was pale, hard, and severe. But suddenly he began to cry. [. . .] 'Is it not terrible that such a thing must happen?' " (B, 166f.).

Felice came to visit Kafka in Zürau, traveling thirty hours to see him. He felt he should have prevented her. "As I see it, she is suffering the utmost misery and the guilt is essentially mine. [. . .] In single details she is wrong, wrong in defending what she calls—or what are really—her rights, but taken all together, she is an innocent person condemned to extreme torture; I am guilty of the wrong for which she is being tortured, and am in addition the torturer" (DII, 184f.).

The engagement was dissolved. On October 16, Kafka wrote his last letter to Felice. He no longer felt that they belonged together and, certainly, no longer saw for them a common future.

After the death of her husband in 1955, Felice decided to accept the proposal of Schocken Books to sell her collection of Kafka letters. Invited by the publisher, she came to New York with the package of Kafka's original correspondence. It was my privilege to negotiate the transfer of this valuable collection. The meeting was quite strange. Mrs. Marasse (her married name) was rather sad to have to part with the letters that for many years were her companions. I tried to persuade her that, once published, the letters would reach many, many readers for whom Kafka has an important message. A new generation was growing up, and it was her duty to help in this process. We talked about Kafka, whom she called a saint: *"Mein Franz war ein Heiliger"* ("My Franz was a saint"). Receding into the last years with Kafka, she reenacted the scene of their parting, at end of December 1917. Kafka shook her hand, which followed her mysteriously as she moved toward the door. She cried now as she cried when she took leave of her Franz. I brought her to the door. She had one more question: "How is Odradek?"—that strange something that is neither a dead object nor a living creature. The question puzzled me. All I could say was, "Please reread 'The Cares of a Family Man,' " the Kafka story in which this something appears. She had one more worry: In the packet of letters there was an envelope containing ones that, in Felice's view, were too intimate for publication; the publisher should promise to treat them confidentially. I had no authority to make this promise and had her contact the publisher. He, however, produced a group of letters which Felice recognized as having been written by Grete Bloch, her antagonist and Kafka's beloved in the period when he was engaged to marry Felice. The publisher sternly requested and received a free hand in dealing with both collections. In the forthcoming critical-historical edition of Kafka's works, all letters will appear in strict chronological order; here Felice and Grete will meet again in a friendly embrace.

In March 1919, Felice married a successful Berlin businessman. Max Brod broke the news gently to Franz. "He was moved, full of the most sincere good wishes for the new marriage, wishes that then to his great joy were fulfilled" (B, 167). Felice Bauer Marasse died in California on October 15, 1960.

Grete Bloch, after the death of her employer in 1936, moved to Italy, where she opened a boarding house in Florence. The British Red Cross reported (May 16, 1945) that she was taken away from Frosinone (Italy) by the Germans in May 1944 and killed by a Nazi soldier.

Julie Wohryzek

In January 1919, Kafka went to Schelesen, in the Italian Tyrol. At the Pension Stüdl, he met Julie Wohryzek, who had come to recuperate from an illness. She was the daughter of a shoemaker and synagogue custodian. Kafka entered into a friendship that developed into an intimate relationship. His letters to her are no longer extant, and the diary for 1919 does not offer much information. We know, however, that Kafka made it clear to Julie that he would not be able to marry her, though he considered marriage and children "the most highly desirable things on earth" (L, 216).

He describes Julie in a letter to Max Brod. She is "a common and yet astounding phenomenon. Not Jewish and yet not not-Jewish, not German and yet not not-German, crazy about the movies, about operettas and comedies, wears face powder and veils, possesses an inexhaustible and nonstop store of the brashest Yiddish expressions, in general very ignorant, more cheerful than sad—that is about what she is like. If one wanted to classify her racially, one would have to say that she belonged to the race of shopgirls. And withal she is brave of heart, honest, unassuming— such great qualities in a person who though not without beauty is as wispy as the gnats that fly against my lamp. In this and other traits resembling Fräulein Grete Bl[och], whom perhaps you remember with aversion. Could you lend me for her [a copy of your] *The Third Phase of Zionism* or some other work that you consider appropriate? She will not understand it, she will not be interested, I will not press it upon her—but anyway" (L, 213).

After closer observation and second thought, Kafka was to revise his critical opinion of Julie. The lady had read a work on Zionism and understood it in her own way. Her fiancé, who had been killed in the war, was a Zionist; her sister attended Judaic lectures; her best friend was a member of the Zionist youth movement—and never missed a lecture by Max Brod (L, 214).

Still, Kafka did not change his mind about Julie's lack of education and her love for popular entertainments. Her attractiveness remained unchallenged, but was this sufficient for a relationship that soon led to thoughts about marriage? Vulgar expressions—Yiddish or otherwise—were fine for the moment, but what about her language in general?

Initially the two could only laugh together, and they did this without stopping. The intimacy did not go beyond holding hands, possibly a bit longer than the custom of the time suggested. They addressed each other using the formal plural ("*Sie*"). Sure enough, the talks came to the problem of marriage. Kafka informed Julie that, despite his high opinion of marriage and children, he could not possibly marry.

At the beginning of March, Julie returned to Prague. Kafka followed her three weeks later. The two met as great lovers would meet. We don't know enough to follow the development of the relationship of these two so different personalities. But in summer we hear of the engagement of Kafka and Julie and of a plan to marry in November. "I had to insist on marriage," he wrote to Julie's sister (L, 218). "We were (and are) so close to each other, closer than J. herself realizes." "It was going to be a love-marriage, but even more a marriage of prudence in the higher sense."

The attitude of Julie's family was "almost touchingly delicate

[. . .] compared with the somewhat coarse though of course very well meant actions of [Kafka's] father" (L, 218). Kafka may not have realized it, but for Mr. Wohryzek, the *shammes*, this was to be an upward marriage, while the Kafkas saw their Franz taking a step downward. If Kafka did realize their relative positions in the social scale, he did not care. What did mean much to him was the simplicity of Julie as compared to his previous loves.

Kafka's father was most outspoken in rejecting his son's choice, Kafka informs us in his "Letter to His Father," written in Schelesen in November 1919. Father Kafka ridiculed his son for following his cheap sexual leanings. "She probably put on a fancy blouse, something these Prague Jewesses are good at, and right away, of course, you decided to marry her. And that as fast as possible, in a week, tomorrow, today. I can't understand you: after all, you're a grown man, you live in the city, and you don't know what to do but marry the next-best girl. Isn't there anything else you can do? If you're frightened, I'll go with you [to the brothel] to see her" (LF, 107). A more vulgar, coarse, ugly, insulting address by a father can hardly be imagined.

It was not to please the father that the marriage did not come about. Kafka discussed the complicated issue in a most subtle, lengthy letter to a married sister of Julie's (L, 215ff.).

Julie had, says Kafka, "a vague longing for glamour, the world, pleasure"; "she scarcely had anything left of her original longing for children." The deep differences between the two suggested that they give up the plan to marry. Kafka maintained that the parting was acceptable to him only because he hoped there was "a reasonable prospect of J.'s marrying, and fairly soon, some good man whom she is willing to accept, having children, and living with him as purely and decently as is possible for ordinary people in our situation." But Kafka also held that Julie could "be content with fidelity or love outside marriage, or what is called marriage nowadays." "If these conditions cannot be fulfilled [. . .], then please leave us to ourselves, for we feel we belong together despite all my frailties."

In addition to the internal problems, there came a practical difficulty: the apartment Kafka and Julie were promised became unavailable and there was no prospect of another place to live. The engagement, which lasted one year, ended in the summer of 1920.

Regrettably, there is no additional information on this friendship. Julie opened a ladies' hatshop in Prague.

Milena Jesenská

Technically, Kafka was still a man engaged to marry when he met Milena Jesenská, a Czech writer and translator. She had requested Kafka's permission to translate some of his stories into Czech. That was sometime in 1920. Kafka, thirty-seven, was in Meran seeking relief for his lung disease; Milena, a twenty-four-year-old woman of unusual intelligence, charm, and love of life, was unwell at the time. Possibly in connection with his stories, Kafka, who barely knew Milena, wrote to her. A friendship developed that lasted several years.

The letters to Milena have been preserved, though not completely. They were not dated; references to certain historical dates point occasionally to the date of a given letter. An attempt to establish the sequence of the letters was made by the publisher for the 1953 edition.

The friendship between Kafka and Milena had humble beginnings. "It occurs to me that I can't remember your face in any precise details. Only how you finally walked away between the tables of the coffeehouse, your figure, your dress, these I can still see" (M, 19). Soon he learned to love her lovely face, her beautiful hands.

Milena was married to Dr. Ernst Polak, a member of the Vienna circle of intellectuals. The marriage was an unhappy one; nevertheless, Milena felt that she "belonged" to her husband and rejected a dissolution of the marriage. Kafka, who knew Polak superficially, had a more positive view of him. "Of your husband I had made myself another picture. In the coffeehouse circle he appeared to me as the most reliable, most understanding, the calmest person, almost exaggeratedly paternal, though also inscrutable, yet not to a point that would cancel what I've just said" (M, 36).

As the relationship grew, Kafka wished to reassure Milena that Dr. Polak did not stand in the way of his wife's friendship with Kafka, just as Kafka was not in the way of Milena's marriage. Milena had written to Kafka in Czech: "Yes, you are right, I love him. But Franz, I love you, too." Kafka's reply: "I'm reading this sentence very carefully, each word, particularly over the 'too' I stop short. Everything is right, you wouldn't be Milena if it weren't right, and where would I be if you didn't exist. [. . .] And yet, out of some weakness, I can't come to terms with the sentence; it's an endless reading and I'm writing it down once more so that you can also look at it and we can read it together, temple to temple. (Your hair against my temple.)" (M, 97). We must assume that Milena understood that her lover could not possibly be satisfied with "I love you, too," regardless of her feelings for Polak.

Kafka respected Dr. Polak for his intelligence and literary skills. As in the case of other persons, Kafka overestimated him. "If only I could talk to him! But I'm afraid of him, he's very superior to me. You know, Milena, when you went to him you took a large step down from your level, but if you come to me you'll leap into the abyss" (M, 60).

Milena's husband's infidelity was known to all in Vienna's and Prague's literary circles without arousing much outrage. Kafka to Milena: "What importance has this 'infidelity' which, moreover, never stops pouring forth deepest happiness even in your deepest grief? What importance has this 'infidelity' compared to my eternal bondage?" (M, 177).

"You [. . .] have not betrayed him, for you love him, whatever you may say, and if we should unite [. . .] it would be on another level, not within his domain" (M, 90). "When you say you love your husband so much (as is also true) that you can't leave him (if only for my sake, I mean: it would be terrible for me if you did it in spite of it) I believe it and agree with you. When you say that although *you* could leave him, he nevertheless needs you inwardly and can't live without you, and that therefore you can't leave him, then I believe it too and also agree with you. But when you say that outwardly he can't cope with life without you and that you therefore (making this a main reason) can't leave him, then this is said either to cover up the above-mentioned reasons [. . .] or else it's one of those pranks of the brain [. . .] under which the body, and not only the body, wriggles" (M, 162).

Milena inquired about Kafka's marital situation. Kafka replied: "I've been engaged twice (three times, if you wish, that's to say, twice to the same girl), so I've been separated three times from marriage by only a few days. The first one [Felice Bauer] is completely over (I hear there's already a new marriage and a small boy), the second is still alive but without any prospect of marriage, so that it actually doesn't live or rather it lives an independent life at the expense of human beings. In general, I've found in this and in other cases that men suffer perhaps more, or if one wants to look at it that way, have less resistance in this respect, but that women always suffer innocently and actually not in the sense that they are 'not at fault,' but in the most real sense which, however, leads once more perhaps to 'not being at fault.' But to reflect on these things is useless" (M, 24f.).

When the relationship between Kafka and Milena grew in

depth, the former attempted to define this closeness. "I kept wanting to hear a different phrase, this one: 'You are mine? And why just that? It doesn't even mean love, rather closeness and night" (M, 182). Or, another time: "You had [. . .] three possibilities in relation to me. You could for instance have told me nothing about yourself, but then you would have deprived me of the pleasure of getting to know you and, what is even more important, of the pleasure of testing myself on it. This is why you didn't dare keep it from me. Then you could have kept a number of things secret or glossed over them and could do so even now, but at the present state of affairs I would feel this even if I didn't mention it and it would hurt doubly. So this you didn't dare do, either. There remains then only the third possibility: to try and protect yourself a little. A small effort does show itself in your letters. Frequently I read of calm and fortitude, also recently often of other things, too, and in the end even of 'real horror' " (M, 31).

Kafka considered himself less and less important, especially when thinking of Milena. He signs one of his letters simply "Thine" and explains in parenthesis: "Now I've lost even my name, it has been growing shorter all the time and now it is: Thine" (M, 67).

"My relationship to you I know (you belong to me even if I were never to see you again)—I know it insofar as it doesn't belong to the unfathomable realm of fear, but your relationship to me I don't know at all, it belongs entirely to fear. Neither do you know me, Milena, I repeat that.

"For me, you see, what's happening is something prodigious. My world is tumbling down, my world is building itself up, watch out how you (this is me) survive it. The tumbling I don't deplore [. . .] but what I do deplore is the building up of it" (M, 71).

At some point (we don't know what point), the Kafka–Milena friendship became a warm, intimate, passionate love. For Milena, love meant the deepest expression of being human. "You know nothing of a person before having been in love with him (or her)," Margarete Buber-Neumann recalls Milena as saying. Such knowledge existed between Kafka and Milena.

Early in the correspondence, Kafka gives Milena exact details about his lung ailment, against the background of her own disease. "Not that I'm particularly alarmed by the disease; probably, and let's hope—your hints seem to suggest this—it is showing itself gently in your case and even a real disease of the lung [. . .], which I've known from my own experience for 3 years, has brought me more good than bad. With me it began about 3 years ago, in the middle of the night with a hemorrhage. I got up, stimulated as one is by anything new [. . .], also somewhat alarmed of course, walked to the window, leaned out, walked to the washstand, walked about the room, sat down on the bed—all the time blood. However, I wasn't in the least unhappy about it, because by degrees I knew for a definite reason that after 3, 4 almost sleepless years I would, provided the hemorrhage stopped, sleep for the first time. It did stop [. . .] and I slept the rest of the night. In the morning though, the maid came in [. . .], a good, almost self-sacrificing but most matter-of-fact girl, saw the blood and said: 'Herr Doktor, you won't last much longer!' But I felt better than usual, went to the office, and to the doctor not until the afternoon.

"The rest of the story, however, is of no importance. I only meant to say: It's not your disease that alarms me [. . .] but the thought of what must have preceded this disturbance. [. . .] What happened was that the brain could no longer endure the burden of worry and suffering heaped upon it. It said: 'I give up; but should there be someone still interested in the maintenance of the whole, then he must relieve me of some of my burden and things will still go on for a while.' Then the lung spoke up, though it probably hadn't much to loose anyhow. These discussions be-

Milena Jesenská
Photograph courtesy of Klaus Wagenbach

tween brain and lung which went on without my knowledge may have been terrible" (M, 21f.).

"I'm mentally ill, the disease of the lung is nothing but an overflowing of my mental disease" (M, 53).

Milena's health also concerned Kafka: "What you say about your health (mine's all right, only my sleep is bad in the mountain air) doesn't satisfy me. The doctor's diagnosis I don't find over-whelmingly favorable, or rather it is neither favorable nor unfavorable, only your reaction can determine how it should be interpreted. Certainly doctors are stupid, or rather they are not more stupid than other people but their pretensions are ridiculous, nevertheless one has to count with the fact that they become more and more stupid the moment one is in their hands and what the doctor demands for the moment is neither very stupid nor impossible. What is impossible is that you become really ill and this impossibility shall remain. In what way has your life changed since you talked to the doctor? This is the main question" (M, 31).

"So the thought of death frightens you? I'm terribly afraid only of pains. This is a bad sign. To want death but not the pains is a bad sign. But otherwise one can risk death. One has just been sent out as a biblical dove, has found nothing green, and slips back into the darkness of the ark" (M, 208).

Taking another tack, Kafka instructs his friend: "To begin with [. . .], lie down in a garden and extract from the disease, especially if it's not a real one, as much sweetness as possible. There's a lot of sweetness in it" (M, 25). Milena recovered.

Milena's character fascinated Kafka. He writes to her: "It is the peculiarity of your being unable to make anyone suffer. It's not by any means out of pity that you can't make people suffer, but just because you're unable to. No, this is fantastic, almost all afternoon I've thought about it, but now I don't dare write it down, perhaps the whole thing is a more or less highfalutin excuse for an embrace" (M, 139). No such praise is found in Kafka's writing or speaking to Felice. On the contrary. Willingly or unwillingly, Felice was the source of much of her friend's suffering, and Kafka often felt that he, unwillingly, brought suffering to Felice.

"Milena, for me you are not a woman, you are a girl, as real a one as I ever saw, I don't think I'll dare offer you my hand, girl, this dirty, twitching, clawlike, unsteady, uncertain, hot-cold hand" (M, 71). Then, most touchingly, "Please stay with me always!" (M, 83).

More and more Milena becomes a factual presence in Kafka's life. "I'm just walking around here between the lines [of his letter], under the light of your eyes, in the breath of your mouth as in a beautiful happy day, which remains beautiful and happy, even when the head is sick, tired" (M, 44). "You're standing firmly near a tree, young, beautiful, your eyes subduing with their radiance the suffering world" (M, 47). "Meanwhile I had the chance to observe you a little, as a matter of fact it made no difference to me what you looked like, the only thing that mattered was your word" (M, 63).

The pessimist Kafka longed for happiness; he thought he had found it in his love for Milena. In the margin of a letter to her: "In spite of everything I sometimes believe: If one can perish from happiness, then this must happen to me. And if a person designated to die, can stay alive through happiness, then I will stay alive" (M, 85). The lover has nothing but his love; in turn his love possesses him: "I somehow can no longer write of anything but what concerns us, us in the turmoil of the world, just us. Everything else is remote. Wrong! Wrong! But the lips are mumbling and my face lies in your lap" (M, 86).

"Until recently I thought I couldn't endure life, couldn't endure people, and was very ashamed of it, but you confirm to me now that it wasn't life that seemed unendurable to me" (M, 105).

"I won't tell you anything but just seat you in the armchair (you said you hadn't been kind enough to me, but could there be more love and honor conferred on me than for you to sit there and let me sit in front of you and be with you). So now I'm seating you in the armchair and don't know how to grasp this happiness with words, eyes, hands, and the poor heart, the happiness that you are here and that you belong to me. And perhaps it isn't you at all I really love, but the existence presented to me by you" (M, 96).

Kafka takes pleasure in comparing himself to his friends: "One peculiarity I think we have in common, Milena: We are so shy and anxious, almost each letter is different, almost each one is frightened by the preceding letter and even more so by the reply. You aren't like this by nature, that's easy to see, and I, perhaps even I, am not like this by nature, but it has almost become my second nature already, it disappears only in despair and sometimes in anger and, needless to say: in fear" (M, 46). Kafka's self-criticism is correct; not so his interpretation of Milena's strong character.

A lover, even one most certain of his beloved, begs to be reassured. To lose the beloved may offer a constant threat to the most intimate relationship. Kafka to Milena: "And write to you I must, Milena, because you could conclude from my last lamenting letters [. . .] that I have grown unsure of you, that I was afraid to lose you. No, I am not unsure, for could you be to me what you are if I were not sure of you? What caused this feeling in me was the brief physical closeness and the sudden physical separation. [. . .] That may after all confuse the senses a bit. Forgive me! And now in the evening as a Goodnight receive the flow of everything I am and have and everything that is blissfully happy to rest in you" (M, 88).

"One evening you wrote that everything might be possible except my losing you—actually only a slight pressure was needed and the impossible would have happened. And perhaps this pressure was actually here and perhaps it did happen" (M, 159).

Did Kafka think he and Milena would ever truly live together?

"It sometimes seems to me that instead of ever living together, we'll just be able contentedly to lie down beside one another in order to die. But whatever happens, it will be close to you" (M, 98). "What an easy life it will be when we are together—fancy writing about it, fool that I am! [. . .] Try to understand me and keep me in your heart" (M, 101f.).

But, later: "Why, Milena, do you write about a common future which after all will never be, or is this why you write about it? [. . .] Few things are certain, but this is one of them: We shall never live together, in the same apartment, body to body, at the same table, never, not even in the same town" (M, 207f.).

"No, Milena, the possibility of a shared life which we thought we had in Vienna, does not exist, under no condition, it didn't even exist then, I had looked 'over my fence,' had just held on to the top with my hands, then I fell back again with lacerated hands. There are of course other possibilities of sharing, the world's full of possibilities, but I don't know them yet" (M, 214f.).

A meeting of the two was discussed in their correspondence. The difference in wording is important. "We're going to see one another earlier than I think? (I write 'see,' you write 'live together.') But I believe (and see it everywhere confirmed, everywhere, in things which have nothing to do with it, all things speak for it) that we never will or can live together, and 'earlier' than 'never' is again only never" (M, 210).

Kafka was deeply conscious of the fact that he was a Jew and Milena a Christian, though neither followed the rituals and tradition of the respective faiths. Kafka knew well that as a Jew he was much older than his thirty-eight years on the calendar; there is a long history and a destiny of many centuries that has to be added to the count. The West European Jew had shaken off the burden of tradition. But Kafka does not—at least with part of his being—consider himself as belonging to that traditionless, uprooted community.

About a hundred East European Jewish refugees who escaped from the advancing Russian armies were housed in the Jewish Town Hall, waiting for American visas. Kafka observed this miserable, suffering humanity. "If I'd been given the choice to be what I wanted, then I'd have chosen to be a small East European Jewish boy in the corner of the room, without a trace of worry[. . .]—and in a few weeks one will be in America. [. . .] There were enough boys like this running around, clambering over the mattresses, creeping under chairs and lying in wait for the bread which someone—they are *one* people—was spreading—with something—everything is edible" (M, 196). "One people" is a biblical term that came to denote the physical and religious oneness of the Jewish people. To be a Jew means to identify with the destiny that this implies and to accept the moral obligation of mutual assistance and help. Kafka, the Western Jew, was aware of this.

"In the evening I talked again to a Palestinian Jew. I believe it's impossible in a letter to make you understand his importance for me—small, almost tiny, weak, bearded, one-eyed man. But the memory of him has cost me half the night" (M, 121). Easily rejecting the assimilated yet only superficially cultured West European Jew, Kafka realized the worth of a person representing the poor, simple, unassuming East European Jew, or one originating there. Kafka, immersed in Western culture, could not be expected to offer a solution to the dilemma, but he could point to the problem and its profundity. It was a serious personal problem.

On a more playful note, he wrote to Milena of his bar mitzvah. At age thirteen, a Jewish boy becomes a bar mitzvah ("Son of the Commandment"), responsible for his actions. "Do you know, by the way, that you were given to me as a present for my confirmation (there's also something like a Jewish confirmation)? I was born in '83, so was 13 when you were born. The 13th birthday is a special occasion. Up near the altar in the temple I had to recite a piece learned by heart with great difficulty, then at home I had to make a brief speech (also learned by heart). I also received many presents. But I imagine that I was not entirely satisfied, one particular present I missed. I demanded it from heaven; it hesitated until August 10" (M, 171). Strange, meaningful imagery, yet typical of Kafka: baby Milena as a bar mitzvah present for the early-maturing boy Franz! Later, again in Kafka's view, Milena grew to be the "guardian angel of Jews" (M, 81).

Still, Kafka truthfully confessed his distance from the Eastern culture he exalted. "We both know, after all, enough typical examples of Western Jews. I am, as far as I know, the most typical Western Jew among them. This means, expressed with exaggeration, that not one calm second is granted me, nothing is granted me, everything has to be earned, not only the present and the future, but the past too—something after all which perhaps every human being has inherited, this too must be earned, it is perhaps the hardest work. When the earth turns to the right—I'm not sure that it does—I would have to turn to the left to make up for the past. But as it is, I haven't the least particle of strength for these obligations. I can't carry the world on my shoulders, can barely stand my winter overcoat on them" (M, 219).

Milena apparently sent Kafka some corrections for the Czech translation of "The Stoker," the first chapter of the novel *Amerika*. Kafka replied: "I'm glad to be able to make a small sacrifice with the few remarks you suggested about 'The Stoker,' it will be a foretaste of that eternal damnation which consists in having to go once more through one's life with the eye of knowledge, wherein the worst is not the insight into obvious misdeeds but into those deeds one once considered to be good" (M, 29).

Kafka's view of human goodness? "My misfortune is that I

consider all human beings—and of course above all those who appear to me the most eminent—to be good; with my reason, with my heart I consider them to be good" (M, 143).

Among biblical motives, images and stories, Kafka was especially attracted by the tale of the Fall of Man, as narrated in Genesis 3; in his "Aphorisms" (written October 1917 to February 1918), he refers to this story as one that depicts the nature and destiny of man. In a letter to Milena he uses the biblical symbolism to explain a happening in itself not important: "It's as though Eve, having indeed plucked the apple from the tree (sometimes I believe I understand the Fall of Man as no one else), did so nevertheless only in order to show it to Adam—because she liked it. It was the biting into it that was decisive—the playing with it was, though not permitted, not forbidden either" (M, 178).

"What you write about the people, Milena, who haven't got the strength to love was correct, even though while writing it down you didn't consider it correct. Perhaps their talent for love consists only in the ability to be loved. And even in this there exists a qualifying distinction for these people. If one of them says to his beloved: 'I believe that you love me,' then this is something different and much less than when he says: 'I'm loved by you.' These, of course, are not lovers but grammarians" (M, 203).

Kafka knew well that true love contains an element of eternity. "I'm tired, can't think of anything and want only to lay my face in your lap, feel your hand on my head and remain like that through all eternity" (M, 108). "Nothing, but to be quiet in your lap" (M, 135). One is reminded of the Song of Songs: "Milena, how good it is to be with you!" (M, 114). Or, in a more modern mode: "Won't you reach out your hand toward me [. . .] and leave it with me for a long, long time?" (M, 115). The contemporary lingo would chose a more direct, more earthy image—which Kafka would have considered impure, even vulgar.

Rarely did Kafka reveal in his writings his innermost attitudes toward "the abyss which he cannot bridge" and toward "all other life" that he has renounced. From a letter: "Since I love you (*and I do love you, you stupid one, as the sea loves a pebble in its depths, this is just how my love engulfs you*—and may I in turn be the pebble with you, if Heaven permits), I love the whole world and this includes your left shoulder—no, it was first the right one, so I kiss it if I feel like it (and if you are nice enough to pull the blouse away from it) and this also includes your left shoulder and your face above me in the forest and my resting on your almost bare breast. And that's why you're right in saying that we were already one and I'm not afraid of it, rather it is my only happiness and my only pride and I don't confine it at all only to the forest. But just between this day-world and that 'half hour in bed' of which you once spoke contemptuously as 'men's business,' there lies for me an abyss which I cannot bridge, probably because I don't want to. [. . .] I have renounced all other life. Look into my eyes!" (M, 136f.).

Another example of Kafka's stress on purity: "I'm dirty, Milena, infinitely dirty, which is why I make so much fuss about purity. No people sing with such pure voices as those who live in deepest hell; what we take for the song of angels is their song" (M, 185f.). "Dirty, infinitely dirty" must be taken as metaphor; in reality, he watched over his cleanliness, physical and emotional. Did he wish to induce Milena to contradict her friend? We don't know.

Kafka enjoyed the playful paradox, half serious, half light-hearted. To Milena: "I remember, for instance, your asking me if I had been unfaithful to you in Prague. It was half joking, half serious, half indifference (again the 3 halves just because it was impossible). You had my letters and yet you asked like that. Was that a possible question? But as if this were not enough, I made it even more impossible. I said, Yes, I had been faithful to you. How can it happen that one talks like this? On that day we talked and

Milena Jesenská
Photograph copyright Giří Gruša; courtesy of S. Fischer Verlag

listened to one another, often and for a long time, like strangers"
(M, 183).

The sad experience that Kafka lived through because of his
dependence on letters in his friendship with Felice, repeated itself
in his relationship with Milena. He realized the possibility of
misunderstandings and the deception inherent in such a relationship, yet could not change his need for letters and telegrams. "Can
I still get a letter by Sunday? It should be possible. But it's crazy,
this passion for letters. Isn't a single one sufficient? Isn't knowing
once sufficient? Certainly it's sufficient, but nevertheless one leans
far back and drinks in the letters and is aware of nothing but that
one doesn't want to stop drinking. Explain this, Milena, teacher!"
(M, 36). "Then came your sweet telegram, a comfort against the
night, that old enemy" (M,48).

"Actually we both write the same things all the time. Now I ask
you if you're ill, then you write about it, now I want to die, then
you, now I want to cry in front of you like a little boy, and then you
in front of me like a little girl. And once and ten times and a
thousand times and all the time I want to be with you and you say
the same. Enough, enough" (M, 135).

Milena complained that, though turned in all directions, some
letters from Kafka were empty, "nothing falls out of them." The
lover's reply: "Yet they are, if I'm not mistaken, just those in which
I feel so close to you, so tamed in my blood and taming yours, so
deep in the forest, so restful in rest, that one doesn't really want to
say anything but that up there through the trees the sky is visible,
that's all, and in an hour one repeats the same thing and indeed
there is in it 'not a single word that isn't very well considered.' It
doesn't last long, either, at most a moment, soon the trumpets of
the sleepless night are blowing again" (M, 46).

"You know after all how I hate letters. All the misfortune of my life [. . .] derives, one could say, from letters or from the possibility of writing letters. [. . .] The easy possibility of letter writing must—seen merely theoretically—have brought into the world a terrible disintegration of souls. It is, in fact, an intercourse with ghosts, and not only with the ghost of the recipient but also with one's own ghost which develops between the lines of the letter one is writing and even more so in a series of letters. [. . .] How on earth did anyone get the idea that people can communicate with one another by letter! [. . .] Writing letters, however, means to denude oneself before the ghosts, something for which they greedily wait. Written kisses don't reach their destination, rather they are drunk on the way by the ghosts. It is on this ample nourishment that they multiply so enormously. Humanity senses this and fights against it and in order to eliminate as far as possible the ghostly element between people and to create a natural communication, the peace of souls, it has invented the railway, the motor car, the airplane. [. . .] After the postal service it has invented the telegraph, the telephone, the radiograph. The ghosts won't starve, but we will perish" (M, 229).

"Then your letter arrived. It's strange nowadays with my writing: you must—when didn't you?—have patience with me. For years I've not written to anyone, in this respect I've been as good as dead, a lack of any desire to communicate, I was as though not of this world but of no other, either" (M, 231).

"These letters after all are nothing but torture, born of torture, incurable torture, create only torture, incurable torture, what's the good of it—and it's getting even worse—during this winter? To be silent, this is the only way to live, here and there. In sadness, all right, what does it matter?" (M, 224).

"You have been agreeing with me for a long time that we should now no longer write to one another. The fact that I happened to be the one to express it is a mere accident, it might just as well have been you. And since we agree on it, it's not necessary to explain why not writing will be good" (M, 224).

"I can't go on writing these letters, not even these important letters. [. . .] I must stop, I can no longer write. [. . .] Please let's not write anymore" (M, 234).

The last extant letter to Milena dates from mid-December 1923. Later on, she visited Kafka several times. In a letter to Brod, Kafka, weakened and in pain, asked him to prevent further visits. Thus ended a deep friendship, one that approached passion, one in which the woman was ready and eager to give more of herself than the beloved was ready (or able?) to accept.

After the relationship had ended, Milena described it in letters to Max Brod: "I knew [Kafka's] terror before I knew him. I armored myself against it by understanding it. In the four days that Franz was with me, he lost it. We laughed at it. [. . .] That was the thing I was able to dispel, that time. When he felt this terror, he looked into my eyes and we waited awhile, just as though we could not catch our breath, or as though our feet hurt, and after a while it passed. Not the slightest exertion was necessary; everything was simple and clear. [. . .] He was simply healthy, and during those days his illness seemed to us something like a minor cold. If I had gone to Prague with him that time, I would have remained what I was to him. But I had sunk both feet so firmly, so infinitely firmly into the ground here; I was not able to leave my husband, and perhaps I was too feminine, too weak, to want to subject myself to this life, which I knew would mean strictest asceticism for life. But there is in me an insuppressible longing, a raging desire for an altogether different kind of life from the one I lead and probably will always lead, for a life with a child, for a life that would be very close to the soil. And probably that weakness won out in me over everything else, over love, over the desire to take flight, over my admiration and again over my life. You know, whatever one tries to say about that, only a lie comes out. This one is perhaps the least of the lies. And then it was already too late. Then this struggle in me came too plainly to the surface, and that frightened him off. For that is the very thing he fought against all his life, from the other side. With me he would have been able to find peace. But then it began to pursue him even with me. Against my will. I knew very well that something had happened which could no longer be thrust aside. I was too weak to do the one and only thing that I knew would have helped him. That *is* my fault. And you too know that it is my fault. The thing that you all call Franz's non-normality— just that is his greatest trait. The women who were with him in the past were ordinary women and did not know how to live except as women. I rather think that all of us, each and every one of us, is sick and that he is the only well person, the only one who sees rightly and feels rightly, the only pure person. I know that he does not resist life, but only this kind of life: that is what he resists. If I had been capable of going with him, he could have lived happily with me. But only now do I know all that. At the time I was an ordinary woman, like all women on the face of the earth, a little instinct-ridden female. Hence his terror. It was perfectly right. [. . .] I know that he loves me. He is too good and chaste to stop loving me. He would feel guilty if he did" (B, 233ff.).

Milena's end came as a victim of the Nazi policy: she was suspected of being a communist and sent to the concentration camp at Ravensbrück, where she died. It is reported that, despite the humiliations inflicted upon her, she behaved as a proud, free human being; she refused to be deprived of her dignity. A few days after Kafka's death, there appeared Milena's obituary of Kafka. She said of her friend that he was "too clear-sighted, too wise, to be able to live." She spoke of "the sensitive vision of a man who observed the world with such distinctness and clarity that he could not bear it and had to die" (*Forum* IX [1962]).

Minze Eisner

While writing the "Letter to His Father," Kafka met Minze Eisner, an eighteen-year-old Bohemian girl who was convalescing from a long illness. She is described as a "young girl, burdened with psychological afflictions and an empty life" (L, 466 n. 19). Kafka felt that he could be of help.

After her departure from Schelesen, a friendly exchange of letters developed. Kafka enjoyed Minze's letters: "You give me great pleasure, really you do, and the days when I received your card and now your letter are distinguished above all others" (L, 243). Minze sent Kafka a picture of herself. In his thanks, Kafka noted "the pensive eyes [. . .], the pensive mouth, the pensive cheeks, everything is pensive; and there is so much to be pensive about in this curious world" (L, 231).

Kafka encouraged his young friend to believe in her better self, to dedicate herself to some useful activity and trust in the worthwhileness of her achievement. He remembers fondly Minze's lovely face and her youthfulness. Youth, he tells her, "dreams of the future and stirs dreams in others, or rather one is oneself a dream, and how could that help being lovely" (L, 225). He made "poor dear Minze" aware of the devil within man which "is neither good nor bad, but is life." "This devil is the material (and basically what wonderful material) that you have been endowed with and with which you are supposed to make something" (L, 229).

An attitude of tenderness and warmth comes through in the short confession: "In case I have not yet said this to you, I shall say it now: you are sweet and good" (L, 238).

In response to one of Minze's letters, one part of which was long and cheerful, the other short and sad, Kafka writes: "The general way of the world [. . .] is neither cheerful nor sad, but even if it momentarily looks cheerful or sad, is always merely a desperate confused mixture." Her friend was happy over her happiness, not so cast down over her sadness. He concludes his letter, "Courage, Minze, courage!" (L, 261f.).

Minze reported a fever with which she awoke every day and remarked sadly, "The faster and more beautifully to squander life, the better." Kafka's answer: "All right, if that's how you want it. But believe me, fever is not a beautiful way to squander life, nor a fast one. [. . .] No one is squandering his life; he is being squandered. But with your fresh youth it is possible to put up a stout fight against it and you must do so" (L, 267).

Kafka quotes Arthur Schopenhauer to clarify the notion that the world and life are always interesting and beautiful, concluding that "this beautiful life in a beautiful world has really to be lived through in every detail of every moment and that is no longer so beautiful, but simply toilsome." Which means that, after a hard day's work, "in the evening, looking into the kerosene lamp at my elbow, it is no longer so beautiful at all and almost to be wept over a little" (L, 267f.).

Thus Kafka tried to teach Minze to appreciate both sides of life and to partake in the work that is to be done. Note the fatherly, mild, caring tone in Kafka's voice. He is glad to see that she is "a little more cheerful" than the last time she wrote (L, 268). He watches her advancement in life. He notes with pleasure that "you

Minze Eisner
Photograph courtesy of Klaus Wagenbach

have not given up before obstacles" and instead "are going forward with your brave and self-reliant life" (L, 363).

In January or February 1923, Minze became engaged. Kafka's last extant letter to her is from March. He asks her to give his regards to her fiancé and to "remain joyous and strong in the great mutation" (L, 369).

Minze died in 1972, at the age of seventy-one. This, too, is a story of love, of a touching, fatherly relationship. And, too, we have here a valuable document of Kafka's philosophy of life.

Dora Dymant

Kafka got to know Dora Dymant at the Baltic resort of Müritz during the summer of 1923. Dora, born in 1902 of an East European hasidic background, was in charge of the kitchen of a children's summer colony belonging to the Berlin Jewish People's Home. At the time, Kafka considered going to Palestine and talked about it to Milena, although it would never have come off; it was pure fantasy. Now, under the influence of the happy life in the children's home, Kafka thought about the possibility of moving to Berlin.

Among the helpers in the Home, Kafka was especially attracted to the young, pretty, charming Dora Dymant. She seemed to him a "wonderful person" (L, 375); he was impressed by her modest, innocent, and mature nature. She felt that this unusual man expected something special from her. They arranged to meet privately. Soon a passionate friendship ensued, and Kafka spent most of his free time with her.

In her memoir of him, Dora identified her attraction for Kafka: "After the catastrophe of the war, everybody was looking to the East for salvation, while I had fled from the East because for me the West was the source of light. Later, my dreams became less demanding. Europe had failed to live up to my expectations, its people were essentially restless. There was something they lacked.

Dora Dymant
Photograph courtesy of Klaus Wagenbach

In the East we knew about the human person; we may have been less at our ease in society, and we may have expressed ourselves less elegantly, but we knew about the essential unity of man and creation. The very first time I saw Kafka I realized that he embodied my conception of what a human being should be. But Kafka also turned to me, as if he expected something from me" (*Der Monat* I [1949]).

The fact that Dora knew Hebrew, especially biblical Hebrew, was an added benefit in this relationship; sometimes she read biblical texts to Kafka. After he and Dora moved to Berlin, Kafka used the library of the Jewish People's Home and attended several lectures at the liberal Academy for Jewish Studies. He enjoyed the scholarly approach to history and literature and the freedom that pervaded discourse and interpretation, so at variance from the old-fashioned mode of Prague. Dora accompanied Kafka whenever possible. It is reported that the masters of the academy disliked the presence of the unmarried couple in their sacred precincts and delegated a younger colleague to convey the message to the strange student. It can be presumed that Kafka, anyway ill, ceased his visits.

Inflation was rampant at the time, food and fuel scarce; dwellings were cold and stomachs empty. Kafka and Dora hesitated to accept food parcels from their parents. People queued up to obtain the meager portions decreed by the authorities. Money lost most of its value. Unemployment was the rule.

Dora took care of most of their day-to-day needs. It became natural for the two lovers to move to one apartment; they found a small one in Berlin-Steglitz. Among their visitors (Kafka had to restrict meeting people) were Puah Bentovim, his early teacher of Hebrew in Prague; the writer Ernst Weiss; Tile Rössler, a girl from the summer camp who became a leading choreographer in Tel Aviv; Kafka's sister Ottla; and Max Brod.

Since Kafka worked at night, he required more lamp oil than

"normal people," which the landlady resented. In order to pacify her Kafka and Dora used the cheapest kind of fuel. Dora prepared food on a methylated-spirit stove or an improvised Dutch oven. Using modern terminology, we could safely say that the two lived "below the poverty line"—or, simply, that they were paupers.

Fantasy knows no limits. When Max Brod visited them, Kafka told his guest of his plan to go to Palestine, where they would open a restaurant with himself as the waiter and Dora as a cook.

At some point in their life together, they decided to get married. Dora informed her father, a devout hasid who, in turn, submitted the plan to his spiritual guide, the Gerer rebbe. No major decision could be made without the rebbe's approval. The man of God read the proposal and uttered just one fateful word: No (for Kafka was not an observant Jew). The two continued their happy life together.

Their happiness was greatly curtailed by Kafka's deteriorating health: high temperature, insomnia, pulmonary fever, and other ills. The doctor's verdict: tuberculosis of the larynx. Kafka was advised to attempt a cure in one of the special sanatoria. Dora took him to the Sanatorium Wiener Wald, but his condition got worse. He became unable to swallow and could only speak in a whisper. Finally, he was taken to the University Hospital in Vienna. There was only an open car to be had, and rain and wind made the trip an ordeal. Dora stood up and tried to protect Kafka with her body.

The next station was the sanatorium at Kierling, a suburb of Vienna. Robert Klopstock, a medical student, interrupted his studies and came to Vienna to be of help to Kafka. He and Dora remained with Kafka to the very end. In order to relieve the larynx, Kafka communicated by writing on slips of paper. One to Dora: "How many years will you be able to stand it? How long will I be able to stand your standing it?" (L, 419). Fearing that Klopstock was withholding his morphine, Kafka wrote, "Don't cheat me; kill me, or you're a murderer" (B, 212). The writer was witty to the very end.

The end came soon. At four o'clock in the morning of June 3, Dora noticed Kafka's heavy breathing and called Klopstock who, in turn, alerted the physician. The end could no longer be delayed. Max Brod tried to reach Dora around midday; it was too late. Kafka lost consciousness and died about noon. As reported by Klopstock, Dora could not stop crying, "My love, my love, my dearest!" (B, 212).

Kafka's parents had wished to visit their son just a few days before his death, but he dissuaded them in a tender and loving letter; he prevented them from seeing their child in a state of pain and deterioration. Thus, only Dora and Klopstock were present at Kafka's death.

The body was brought to the mortuary. Dora cried, "My love, my dearest: he is so alone, yes, so quite alone, there is nothing for us to do, oh my dear one, my sweet." The burial took place Tuesday, June 11, 1924, in the Jewish burial ground in Prague. About one hundred people followed the casket from the hall to the grave. Dora threw herself on the grave, weeping. Her cry was penetrating, painful. The Hebrew prayer of hope for salvation was recited.

How much would Kafka have liked to hear these proclamations of a woman's love—for they were unconditional, pure, and true. Perhaps in the last hours of life he had a premonition that Dora would be the one to declare that he—the lonely one—was more than a thinker, more than a poet, a visionary: he was a lover.

Dora, the most sincere among those assembled at the funeral, represented the warm, simple, caring, loving human being, the one Kafka felt closest to, one to which he could relate without at the same time feeling the tragic opposite, the dreadful paradox of life. Dora's anguished outcry at the open grave said more than could be expressed by eulogies and press notices.

In the announcements of the funeral, the parents stated that they did not wish to receive the customary visits of condolence. It was Kafka who, in the years and decades to come, was to offer solace to an ailing, troubled world. It was he who reminded mankind of the indestructible element which it was about to forget.

Kafka, the last photograph, 1923 or 1924

Chronology

1883	July 3: Born in Prague.
1889–93	Elementary school.
1893–1901	Altstädter Gymnasium.
1896	June 13: Bar mitzvah.
1898	Friendship with Oskar Pollak and Hugo Bergmann.
1899–1903	Early writings (destroyed).
1901–6	German University, Prague. Studies chemistry, then law. Spring 1902, studies German literature.
1902	Summer: Vacation in Liboch and Triesch with Dr. Siegfried Löwy (the "country doctor"). October 23: First meeting with Max Brod.
1904–5	Autumn–winter: Writes "Description of a Struggle" (first version).
1905	July–August: Vacation in Zuckmantel. First love affair.
1906	April–September: Clerk in a law office. June 18: Doctor of law degree. August: Vacation in Zuckmantel. Love affair. October: Beginning of one-year legal training.
1907	October: Starts job at Assicurazioni Generali in Prague.
1908	March: First publication (eight short pieces in *Hyperion*). July: Starts job at Workers' Accident Insurance Institute for the Kingdom of Bohemia in Prague.
1909	March: Publication of two sections from "Description of a Struggle" in *Hyperion*.

September: Vacation in Riva and Brescia with Max Brod. Writes and publishes (in *Bohemia*) "The Aeroplanes at Brescia."

1910   Begins to keep diary.
March: Publication of five pieces in *Bohemia*.

1911   January–February: Beginning of travel diaries.
Summer: Vacation (with Max Brod) to Lugano, Stresa, Milan, Paris. Then alone to sanatorium near Zurich.
October 4: Attends a performance of an East European Yiddish troupe, followed by many more through the winter. Friendship with the actor Yitzhak Levy.
Winter: Working on first version of *Amerika*.

1912   February 18: Evening of recitations of Yitzhak Levy (organized and introduced by Kafka).
June–July: Meets Ernst Rowohlt and Kurt Wolff. Sanatorium in the Harz Mountains.
August 13: Meets Felice Bauer.
September 22–23: Writes "The Judgment" overnight.
September–October: Writes "The Stoker"; begins second version of *Amerika*.
November–December: Writes *The Metamorphosis*.
December 4: Gives public reading of "The Judgment."
December: *Meditation* published by Rowohlt.

1913   January 18: Meets Martin Buber.
January 24: Interrupts writing of *Amerika*.
Easter: With Felice in Berlin.
April: Gardening work in Troja, near Prague.
May 11–12: With Felice in Berlin.
May: *The Stoker* published by Kurt Wolff.
June: "The Judgment" published in *Arkadia*.
June 28: Meets Ernst Weiss.
September–October: In Vienna to attend International Congress on Accident Prevention; Zionist Congress. In Riva; relationship with G.W., "the Swiss girl."
November 8–9: With Felice in Berlin.

1914   February 28–March 1: In Berlin with Felice.
Easter: In Berlin. Unofficial engagement to Felice.
May 1: Felice in Prague. Search for apartment.

May 30–June 2: In Berlin. Official engagement to Felice.
July 12: In Berlin. Engagement broken.
August: Begins work on *The Trial*.
September: Moves to his sister Elli's apartment.
October: Takes leave of absence to work on *The Trial*; writes last chapter of *Amerika* and "In the Penal Colony." Correspondence with Felice.
December: Writes "The Village Schoolmaster ["The Giant Mole"] (unfinished).

1915   January 17: Stops work on *The Trial*.
January 23–24: With Felice in Bodenbach.
January–February: Writes "Blumfeld, an Elderly Bachelor" (unfinished).
April: To Hungary with Elli.
May 23–24: With Felice Bauer and Grete Bloch in Bohemian Switzerland.
June: With Felice in Karlsbad.
July: In a sanatorium in Rumburg (Northern Bohemia).
October: *The Metamorphosis* published in *Die weissen Blätter*.
November: Book publication of *The Metamorphosis*.

1916   April: Official trip to Karlsbad (with his sister Ottla).
July 3–12: With Felice in Marienbad; with Felice to Franzensbad; then alone at Marienbad.
October: "The Judgment" published in book form.
November 10–12: In Munich, meets with Felice; reads "In the Penal Colony" at Gallery Goltz.
November 26: Begins to write the stories in *A Country Doctor*.

1916–17   Winter: Writes "The Warden of the Tomb."

1917   March: Continues to write at Ottla's home on Alchimistengasse.
Spring: Writes "An Imperial Message" (as part of the story "The Great Wall of China") and "The Hunter Gracchus."
Summer: Begins to learn Hebrew. Writes "A Report to an Academy."
July: Felice in Prague; second engagement. With Felice in Hungary; returns alone, stopping in Vienna. "An Old

Manuscript" and "A Fratricide" published in *Marsyas*.
August 9–10: Hemorrhage of the lung.
September: Moves into his parents' apartment. Doctor diagnoses tuberculosis of the lungs. Three months' sick leave; joins Ottla in Zürau (until April 1918).
September 20–21: Felice in Zürau.
October: "Jackals and Arabs" published in *Der Jude*. To Komotau and Prague for a few days with Max Brod and Ottla.
November: "A Report to an Academy" published in *Der Jude*.
December (last week): To Prague. Felice in Prague; second engagement broken off.

1918   April: Leaves Zürau, returns to Prague.
May: Resumes work at the Institute.
Summer: Gardening work in Troja.
Mid-October–late November: Ill with Spanish influenza; sick again after a few days back at work.
November 30–December: In Schelesen; then in Prague.

1919   January 22: Returns to Schelesen; meets Julie Wohryzek.
May: "In the Penal Colony" published in book form.
Summer: Engagement to Julie Wohryzek.
Autumn: Publication of *A Country Doctor*. Takes Hebrew lessons from Friedrich Thieberger.
October (end): Receives first letter from Milena Jesenská-Polak.
November: Wedding with Julie Wohryzek scheduled for November 2 or 9, but postponed because of apartment problems. With Max Brod to Schelesen. Meets Minze Eisner. Writes "Letter to His Father."
November 21: Returns to Prague and the office.

1919–20   Winter: Recurrent illness.
1920   January: Begins writing *He* (aphorisms).
April: To Meran. Correspondence with Milena.
June 27–July 4: In Vienna; four days with Milena.
July: Breaks engagement to Julie Wohryzek, but continues seeing her. Returns to work. Lives at Elli's apartment.
August 8: Moves back to his parents' apartment.
August 14–15: Meets Milena in Gmünd.

August (end): Resumes his literary work after more than three years of inactivity.

December: To Matliary in the High Tatra Mountains (until August 1921).

1921   January: Tries to break off with Milena.

March (end): Gravely ill.

August (end): Returns to Prague; resumes job at Institute.

September–October: Milena in Prague; Kafka gives her his diaries.

October 15: Resumes diary entries.

October 31: Sick leave to undergo special treatment.

November: Several visits by Milena.

1922   February: Writes "A Hunger Artist." Begins work on *The Castle.*

April–May: Visits by Milena.

June: To Planá.

July: Pensioned by the Institute (he had not worked since October 1921). Writes "Investigations of a Dog."

August 20: Stops work on *The Castle.*

October: Publication of "A Hunger Artist" in *Die Neue Rundschau.*

November–December: Mostly in bed.

December 2: Ludwig Hardt reads works by Kafka in Prague.

December: Hebrew lessons from Puah Bentovim.

1923   Winter–spring: Mostly bedridden. Continues Hebrew lessons.

June: Last meeting with Milena.

July–August: In Müritz on the Baltic with Elli and her children. Meets Dora Dymant. Returns to Prague via Berlin.

Mid-August–September: With Ottla in Schelesen.

September 24: To Berlin to live with Dora. Studies Hebrew.

October–December: Writes "A Little Woman" and "The Burrow."

November 15: Moves with Dora to Grunewaldstrasse 13.

November–December: Attends lectures at Academy for Jewish Studies.

December (end): Bedridden with fever.

1924   February: Moves with Dora to Heidestrasse 25–26 in

Zehlendorf. Health declines rapidly.

Mid-March: Max Brod comes to Berlin, takes Kafka back to Prague. Writes "Josephine the Singer, or the Mouse Folk."

March (end): Dora comes to Prague; takes Kafka to Sanatorium Wiener Wald on April 7.

April: With Dora in Sanatorium Wiener Wald. Tuberculosis of the larynx.

Mid-April: Briefly at Professor M. Hajek's clinic in Vienna. Dora accompanies Kafka to Dr. Hoffmann's Sanatorium in Kierling. "Josephine" published in the *Prager Presse*.

May: Robert Klopstock joins Dora in nursing Kafka. Kafka corrects part of the galleys of A *Hunger Artist*, published in 1924 after his death.

June 3: Death in Kierling; burial June 11 in the Jewish cemetery in Prague-Strašnice.

June 19: Memorial service at the Little Theater in Prague.

Bibliography

Brod, Max, *Franz Kafka: A Biography*. Translated by G. Humphreys Roberts and Richard Winston. New York, 1960.

Buber-Neumann, Margarete, *Kafka's Friend Milena*. Berlin, 1963.

Canetti, Elias, *Kafka's Other Trial: The Letters to Felice*. Translated by Christopher Middleton. New York, 1974.

Emrich, Wilhelm, *Franz Kafka*. Frankfurt am Main, 1970.

Janouch, Gustav, *Conversations with Kafka*. Translated by Geronwy Rees. New York, 1971.

Franz Kafka, *Diaries: 1910–1913*. Edited by Max Brod, translated by Joseph Kresh. New York, 1948.

————, *Diaries: 1914–1923*. Edited by Max Brod, translated by Martin Greenberg and Hannah Arendt. New York, 1949.

————, *Letters to Felice*. Edited by Erich Heller and Jürgen Born, translated by James Stern and Elisabeth Duckworth. New York, 1973.

————, *Letters to Friends, Family and Editors*. Translated by Richard and Clara Winston. New York, 1977.

————, *Letters to Milena*. Edited by Willi Haas, translated by Tania and James Stern. New York, 1953.

————, *Letters to Ottla and the Family*. Edited by N. N. Glatzer, translated by Richard and Clara Winston. New York, 1982.

Politzer, Heinz, *Franz Kafka: Parable and Paradox*. Ithaca, N.Y., 1962.

Schocken, Wolfgang Alexander. "A Memoir of Grete Bloch." Unpublished.

Acknowledgments

Grateful acknowledgment is extended to the following for permission to reprint material:

Franz Kafka: A Biography by Max Brod, copyright © 1937 by Heinr. Mercy Sohn, Prague; copyright © 1947, 1960, 1963, 1975 by Schocken Books Inc.

Diaries: 1910–1913 by Franz Kafka, copyright © 1948 by Schocken Books Inc. Copyright renewed 1975 by Schocken Books Inc.

Diaries: 1914–1923 by Franz Kafka, copyright © 1949 by Schocken Books Inc. Copyright renewed 1976 by Schocken Books Inc.

Letter to His Father by Franz Kafka, copyright © 1953, 1954, 1966 by Schocken Books Inc.

Letters to Friends, Family, and Editors by Franz Kafka, copyright © 1958, 1977 by Schocken Books Inc.

Letters to Felice by Franz Kafka, copyright © 1967, 1973 by Schocken Books Inc.

Letters to Milena by Franz Kafka, copyright © 1953 by Schocken Books Inc.